Building and Restoring Relationships in Schools

Implementing 'Restorative Practice' in schools can offer powerful and effective methods of promoting harmonious relationships and resolving conflict. Restorative Practice helps disruptive pupils to take responsibility for their actions, understand the consequences of their behaviour and apologize to others. Through a whole-school approach, school teachers and managers can help all children build healthy and respectful relationships with peers and teachers.

Building and Restoring Respectful Relationships in Schools is a practical resource to help relieve the pressure on schools and education services by leading them to plan and implement restorative approaches in their day-to-day work. This innovative and informative book:

- provides a comprehensive overview of the current range of restorative approaches in schools;
- offers a clear framework and theoretical perspective for understanding the range of approaches;
- gives practical examples and case studies to illustrate practice;
- contains practical exercises and other useful resource materials;
- is relevant to individual staff as well as whole schools and education services.

Richard Hendry offers a vision for how our schools can be, if we are willing to embrace a 'way of being' that nurtures personal responsibility in a climate of mutual respect. As well as showing teachers how to reduce disruption and develop good relationships, this book is also about improving learning in schools and building skills for life. *Building and Restoring Respectful Relationships in Schools* is essential reading for all teachers, especially department and year heads, as well as headteachers, policy makers and researchers.

Richard Hendry is Sacro's National Coordinator for Work with Schools, is an associate tutor in postgraduate studies for teachers at Edinburgh University's School of Education and is a course author for the Open University in Scotland.

Building and Restoring Respectful Relationships in Schools

A guide to using Restorative Practice

Richard Hendry

Routledge
Taylor & Francis Group

LONDON AND NEW YORK

First published 2009
by Routledge
2 Park Square, Milton Park, Abingdon, Oxon OX14 4RN

Simultaneously published in the USA and Canada
by Routledge
711 Third Avenue, New York, NY 10017, USA

Routledge is an imprint of the Taylor & Francis Group, an informa business

© 2009 Richard Hendry

Typeset in Sabon by GreenGate Publishing Services

British Library Cataloguing in Publication Data
A catalogue record for this book is available from the British Library

Library of Congress Cataloging-in-Publication Data
Hendry, Richard, 1959–
  Building and restoring respectful relationships in schools: a guide to
  using restorative practice / Richard Hendry.
  p. cm.
  Includes bibliographical references and index.
  1. Problem children—education—Scotland. 2. Problem children—
  Behavior modification—Scotland. 3. Teacher–student relationships—
  Scotland. 4. School discipline—Scotland. I. Title.
  LC4803.G7H46 2009
  371.9309411–dc22   2009000264

ISBN10: 0-415-54398-8 (hbk)
ISBN10: 0-415-54427-0 (pbk)

ISBN13: 978-0-415-54398-9 (hbk)
ISBN13: 978-0-415-54427-6 (pbk)

Contents

Figures

Tables

Acknowledgements

This book can exist only because of the effective collaboration of many practitioners who have developed and implemented Restorative Approaches, and who have contributed to the collective learning on the value of Restorative Practice in schools. I have drawn on this experience through my contact with others in the field, as well as on my own experience as a restorative practitioner, trainer and consultant. In writing this book I want to acknowledge the many practitioners throughout the international education community who continue to add to the collective pool of experience in Restorative Practice. This book is my contribution to that growing pool.

I would particularly like to acknowledge the contributions of:

- Dr Gillean McLuskey (University of Edinburgh) and Jean Kane (University of Glasgow), for their substantial contribution to Chapter 2. Their experience and depth of knowledge in the research and implementation of Restorative Practice were invaluable.
- Ken Keighren (Deputy Principal Educational Psychologist, Fife Council), for his substantial contribution to Chapter 8. His ability to reflect with clarity and insight on the implementation process at education service level informs this chapter. My thanks also go to Fife Council Education Service for permission to reproduce materials.
- Sacro, for the support and opportunities that they have afforded me, and for permission to reproduce materials developed originally for their use. The expertise and experience of their trainers and staff have made a significant contribution to my understanding and therefore to the content of this book. In particular I would thank Tony Brown, Ian McDonough and Billy Nicol.
- Dr Gwynedd Lloyd (University of Edinburgh) led the evaluation team for the Scottish government's pilot of Restorative Practices in Scottish schools. Her support and advice in producing this book were invaluable.
- Lynn Strachan is a primary school headteacher (and my wife) with many years' experience in primary schools' work. She has helped to

ensure that the contents of this book are as relevant to the primary as they are to the secondary (high) school sector. She has also provided editorial support throughout.

I also wish to acknowledge the work of Derek Brookes, Belinda Hopkins, Margaret Jarvie, Carl Rogers and Marg Thorsborne, who have been particularly influential in my thinking and development in this field. Thanks also are due to Tony Finn and the Scottish government's Positive Behaviour Team.

Finally, I thank my parents, without whom this book would not have been possible.

Chapter 1

An introduction to Restorative Practice

This chapter covers:

    When I started teaching
    Change is in the air
    Supporting the development of Restorative Practice
    Terminology
    Ten frequently asked questions

After twenty-five years of sitting in staffrooms, I have learned that when a teacher begins an anecdote with 'When I started teaching…', this does not always guarantee that what follows is worth listening to. And so it is with some trepidation that I begin.

When I started teaching

When I started teaching… a dominant culture among teachers was that of professional individualism. You were alone with your class. The door closed firmly behind you. Whether you swam confidently, struggled to keep your head above water or sank like a stone depended, in the main, on two factors:

- the skills and attitudes that you brought from your previous experiences – in my case mainly from having been a pupil;
- your ability to adapt, and to learn from new experiences.

Of course, the preparation provided by formal teacher training was also a factor. However, this preparation proved woefully inadequate, for me at least, in terms of helping children to relate effectively to others and for dealing with challenging and disturbing behaviour when it arose.

Much has changed in the intervening twenty-five years. That culture of professional individualism has been challenged by a number of factors, including:

- the encouragement of reflective practice through staff development, self-evaluation and peer support programmes;
- increased opportunities for collaborative working between class teachers and support staff in classes;
- moves towards greater professional accountability.

These days, those who work in schools are, perhaps, more willing to share their experiences and skills with colleagues. Indeed, these experiences need to be shared if we are to have meaningful responses to the challenges that teaching throws up.

On the other hand, some things seem to have changed only superficially.

When I started teaching... I had the option of hitting with a leather belt those pupils who did something wrong or who did not behave the way I wanted them to. Proud as I am of my refusal to resort to this punishment, at the time my stance simply reduced by one the very limited number of available options for responding to unacceptable behaviour. When humour, persuasion or reasoned argument failed, all I could resort to were lesser forms of punishment (rows, having the culprit write out lines, or detention), or else I could pass on the 'problem' for someone more senior to deal with.

Since the mid-1990s, teachers have been encouraged, and sometimes directed, to adopt more positive approaches to 'behaviour management'. The threat of sanctions has been 'balanced' by the increased use of praise and concrete rewards. While there is evidence that such behaviourist approaches can bring about changes in the conduct of some pupils, at least on a temporary basis, not everyone is at ease with this approach.

Praise and reward systems have been criticized for being, at best, difficult to administer consistently. At worst, they can be seen as tokenistic and may even be detrimental to a child's developing sense of personal responsibility. Some children simply do not seem to respond to them in the ways intended. Some children learn to 'work the system'. In other contexts, these children might be described as rapid learners, but when we are trying to manage their behaviour through behaviourist approaches, their ability to use the system to get what they want is often perceived as manipulative or underhand. (See Chapter 8 for a more detailed discussion of this issue.)

Despite this apparent shift towards more positive approaches, the threat or actual use of sanctions (retribution) as a way of managing unacceptable behaviour remains a dominant culture in most of our schools. And yet, although sanctions may in some sense bring temporary relief, I cannot say that the need to resort to such retribution ever felt 'right' or 'good' to me when I was meting it out. The evidence of my own experience, as well as that from research, is that such sanctions do little to help children and young people understand their own behaviours or to take responsibility for the impact of those behaviours on others. Experience also tells us that sanctions are least effective for those pupils who are most frequently subjected to them.

These are the very children most in need of constructive support if we are to help them change their behaviours. And yet, this kind of retributive thinking remains a smoke that can cloud our judgement when making decisions about how best to respond to incidents of conflict and harm in schools.

Albert Einstein suggested that one definition of insanity is 'doing the same thing over and over again and expecting a different result'.

Change is in the air

Basic psychology tells us that if we are to have any hope of influencing the behaviours of children, we need to pay attention to their thinking and feeling processes as well as to their overt behaviours. Restorative Approaches do just that: they offer a theoretically coherent and practical basis for our interactions with others, and in doing so provide valid alternatives to our more typically retributive responses to rule breaking and wrongdoing.

We can identify three aspects of our work in schools that allow us to influence students' learning and behaviour (Figure 1.1):

- the content of the curriculum that we teach;
- the behaviours that we as adults model when we relate to others;
- the interventions we choose to use when things go wrong between people, or when people do the wrong thing.

This book will show how Restorative Practice can be adopted in all three of these areas, with a particular focus on intervening in incidents of conflict and harm. This book reflects on international developments in the field and draws particularly on the experience of Scottish schools involved in implementing Restorative Approaches in the first decade of the twenty-first century.

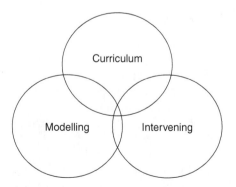

Figure 1.1 Three aspects that influence learning and behaviour

Restorative Justice principles and processes have existed in some cultures for hundreds of years. Some of the restorative processes that are now being used in UK schools have been tried and tested in a number of countries for up to twenty-five years. Schools in the United Kingdom are relative new-comers to Restorative Practice but since around 2000 there has been a burgeoning of development work in many areas.

In Scotland, the government is currently promoting the voluntary development of Restorative Practice in all its schools, building on successful pilots initiated in 2004. It has also made Restorative provision available within the justice system for young people, and in wider community settings. All this makes the Scottish experience particular. Scottish schools have been able to apply ideas and approaches that schools in other countries have previously developed. Scottish practitioners have gleaned information from the experience of others and have built on the learning of others to create models of implementation that work at individual school, cluster group and local authority levels. This book aims to share this recent learning by reflecting on the experience of individual staff members, headteachers, individual schools, local authority education services and Restorative Practice trainers.

When I started teaching... twenty-five years ago, Restorative Practice was not an option for schools. It is now. Evidence from pilot and lead schools in the United Kingdom, supported by evidence from other countries, indicates that schools that effectively adopt Restorative Practice can become significantly safer, calmer and happier places in which to learn and teach. Given the evident failings of our retributive systems and the evident potential of Restorative Practice, we cannot afford to ignore this way of working.

Supporting the development of Restorative Practice

This book will help you to consider how Restorative Practice can bring about lasting positive change in the ways we teach children to communicate constructively, to resolve conflict and to address harm. The book will support the development of Restorative Practice by:

- providing an opportunity for you to reflect on your values and your current responses to conflict and harm, and to compare these values and responses with those of Restorative Practice;
- exploring the existing range of Restorative Approaches and how these can be implemented at school and education service level;
- looking at some real experiences of change in schools, as reported by staff and students.

This book is *not* intended as a substitute for the kind of experiential staff development programmes that are *essential* to the successful implementation of Restorative Practice. It does not aim to provide a full theoretical background to the various processes described. Nor does it aim to convince the sceptical that Restorative Approaches can make a difference. Sources for reading on these aspects of Restorative Practice are given at the end of the book in a section headed 'Resources'.

The book categorizes Restorative Practice into two broad groupings:

- *Proactive approaches.* These are designed to establish the kinds of skills and climate that will build constructive communication and relationships, and will help minimize incidences of conflict and harm in schools.
- *Responsive approaches.* These are interventions that help people to re-establish effective communication, specifically by resolving conflict and/or addressing harm done.

Chapters 2, 3 and 4 will describe the background to Restorative Approaches, the values that underpin them, what it is that they aim to achieve and the contexts in which they can be used. Chapters 5 and 6 will explain in some detail how Restorative Approaches actually work in schools. Chapters 7 and 8 will look at the implications of implementing Restorative Approaches at three levels: individual staff, whole-school and education service levels. Examples of development models are also considered.

Terminology

The use of Restorative Practice in education has developed rapidly and simultaneously in a number of countries. This has inevitably led to variations in the terminology. Figure 1.2 offers a framework for understanding how terms are used in this book.

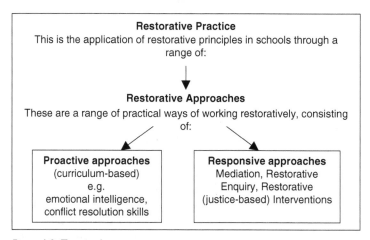

Figure 1.2 Terminology

Ten frequently asked questions

This section is offered as a quick reference point; more detailed explanations and discussions can be found in later chapters. The chapters in which these can be found are indicated at the end of each response. The questions addressed in this section are:

1 What is Restorative Practice?
2 What is being 'restored' in a Restorative Approach?
3 Who can use Restorative Approaches? For instance, are they suitable for very young children?
4 Can I use Restorative Approaches in my school if other staff and the wider school community are not working in this way?
5 Isn't a Restorative Intervention a soft option for the person responsible for causing harm?
6 Can Restorative Approaches be used to address bullying?
7 How can you ensure that people will take part in a Restorative Intervention?
8 If we start using Restorative Approaches, do we have to stop using sanctions?
9 Aren't Restorative Approaches too time-consuming to be used in the classroom?
10 Isn't this just another educational fad that will be dropped after a year or two?

I What is Restorative Practice?

Restorative Practice is a way of working with children that acknowledges the central importance of effective relationships in schools and promotes the school's role in developing these. It places particular emphasis on developing respect, empathy, social responsibility and self-regulation. There are a range of proactive and responsive Restorative Approaches that schools can learn to use. Proactive approaches build emotional intelligence and resilience. Responsive Approaches focus on resolving conflict and addressing wrongdoing and harm (see Chapters 5 and 6).

2 What is being 'restored' in a Restorative Approach?

What is being 'restored' depends on the context and the approach being adopted. A Restorative Approach may focus on some aspect of the individual's self-concept (intrapersonal) or it may focus on some aspect of a particular relationship (interpersonal). In any intervention, one or more of the qualities shown in Table 1.1 may be restored (see Chapters 3 and 4).

Table 1.1 What can be restored?

Interpersonal	Intrapersonal
Effective communication	Self-respect or self-worth
Respect for others	Self-confidence
Understanding another's perspective	Feeling safer
Understanding the impact of one's own behaviour on others	Understanding the consequences of one's own behaviour for oneself
Reparation for material loss or damage	Dignity

3 Who can use Restorative Approaches? For instance, are they suitable for very young children?

With appropriate understanding and training, anyone in the school community can learn to use Restorative Approaches, including school staff (Chapter 7), children, young people and parents. For children to take part meaningfully in a Responsive Intervention (Chapter 6), they need to be able to communicate their feelings and thoughts at a basic level. Schools that embrace Restorative Practice pay particular attention to building the emotional intelligence of their children in proactive ways (see Chapter 5).

4 Can I use Restorative Approaches in my school if other staff and the wider school community are not working in this way?

In any school there will be scope for school staff to work in ways that reflect their individuality. Most children and young people are remarkably good at adapting their responses to the varied approaches of different adults. It is perfectly feasible for an individual teacher to introduce Restorative Practice in isolation. Many teachers will recognize aspects of Restorative Approaches in their current practice. However, we should not underestimate the potential stress for children and staff that can be created by one individual adopting a Restorative Approach in a school climate that is otherwise essentially retributive – or, for that matter, of the reverse scenario. The evidence of individual experience and research indicates that schools that implement Restorative Practice on a genuinely whole-school basis will have the most beneficial impact on their pupils' learning and development in the longer term (see Chapter 8).

5 Isn't a Restorative Intervention a soft option for the person responsible for causing harm?

In our culture, when someone feels wronged or harmed, the need for retribution or even revenge can be strong. Restorative Interventions do not recognize these needs as helpful and so do not aim to meet them. This can be difficult for some people to accept at first. But Restorative Interventions do hold people accountable for their actions and help them to understand the impact of their behaviours on others. Meaningful reparation for harm done is a common outcome. Most people know that facing up to problems or making a genuine apology face to face with the person you have offended is rarely an easy option. Importantly, Restorative Interventions offer real hope of supporting positive changes in people's behaviours that are rarely achieved through other, punitive approaches (see Chapter 3).

6 Can Restorative Approaches be used to address bullying?

The term 'bullying' encompasses a complex range of behaviours, and different people often use the term in different ways. Where one person has clearly harmed another, and is supported in taking responsibility for their actions, a Restorative Intervention may be an effective way of addressing and helping the person to change the behaviour while allowing the person who has been bullied to feel supported (see Chapter 6).

7 How can you ensure that people will take part in a Restorative Intervention?

At the heart of restorative thinking lies the voluntary nature of restorative processes. People can be reluctant to take part in *any* process that addresses conflict or harm because of their previous experiences of ineffective or unhelpful interventions, including sanctions. Skilled Restorative practitioners are able to create a climate that supports voluntary participation. In practice, there are high uptake rates by participants (see Chapters 3 and 6).

8 If we start using Restorative Approaches, do we have to stop using sanctions?

The short answer to the question of whether using Restorative Approaches involves stopping using sanctions is 'No', but this questions is a bit like asking, 'If we start eating healthy foods, do we have to stop eating unhealthy ones?' As participation in Restorative Interventions is voluntary, many schools feel the need to retain the option of sanctions when introducing Restorative Practice. However, the need to resort to sanctions reflects a particular way of thinking about and responding to wrongdoing. This retributive mindset is common but not universal in our culture. Restorative Practice provides a very different way of thinking and acting in response to conflict and harm. Once staff, students and parents understand this, the need and, more importantly, the desire to rely on sanctions can be significantly reduced or even removed (see Chapter 8).

9 Aren't Restorative Approaches too time-consuming to be used in the classroom?

Restorative language can permeate all our interactions. When something goes wrong in class, a Restorative Conversation between a member of staff and a pupil might take as little as two minutes; or it might need a little longer. Interventions for higher-tariff incidents will require some preparation time to be set aside before the people concerned are brought together. Of course, investigative and punitive responses can take time as well, sometimes a great deal of time! However, the real question for staff and schools is, 'Are we willing to invest time in an approach that can bring about real changes for the people involved?' (see Chapters 5 and 6).

10 Isn't this just another educational fad that will be dropped after a year or two?

Restorative Practice has been developing in several countries for around thirty years. Some of its roots lie in cultures that are hundreds of years old. While it is relatively new as a way of working in schools, there is a growing body of research that gives evidence of its effectiveness. Whether it is adopted widely as a way of thinking and working will depend principally on the depth of our desire for more effective ways of working with children and young people in schools. Local authorities and governments can and should support and promote the adoption of Restorative Practice. However, the notion that Restorative Practice could ever become compulsory in schools is antithetical to the principle of voluntary participation that underpins all Restorative Approaches.

Chapter 2

International and UK experiences

Introduction

This chapter aims to review national and international experiences and perspectives on Restorative Practice and to set current thinking about Restorative Approaches in a school context. The chapter covers the following topics:

Where have Restorative Practice ideas come from?
What is Restorative Justice and what does it look like?
How have the ideas of Restorative Justice evolved in schools?
What has been learned so far?
Future development trends

Where have Restorative Practice ideas come from?

Until recently, most of the available background reading on Restorative Practice came from those working to establish Restorative Justice in the field of criminal justice (Zehr 2002; Marshall 1998; Sherman and Strang 1997). There was, and still is, no single universal definition of Restorative Justice, though the following definitions are helpful:

A process whereby all the parties with a stake in a particular offence come together to resolve collectively how to deal with the aftermath of offence and its implications for the future.

(Marshall 1998)

[It] holds the promise of restoring victims' material and emotional loss, safety, damaged relationships, dignity and self-respect.

(Hoyle *et al.* 2002: 101)

The traditional institutional response to offending behaviour in the United Kingdom, and in many other countries, can be described as Retributive Justice. Restorative Justice can be distinguished from Retributive Justice as shown in Table 2.1.

Table 2.1 Retributive and Restorative Justice: two different views of justice

Retributive Justice	Restorative Justice
Crime is a violation of the law and the state.	Crime is a violation of people and relationships.
Violations create guilt.	Violations create obligations.
Justice requires the state to determine blame (guilt) and impose pain (punishment).	Justice involves those responsible for harm, those harmed, and other community members in an effort to put things right.
Central focus is on 'offenders' getting what they deserve.	Central focus is on 'victim's' needs and 'offender's' responsibility for repairing harm.

Source: Adapted from Zehr (1985).

Zehr (1990) also says that Restorative Practice 'is a compass, not a map', by which he implies that, when addressing offending behaviour, Restorative Justice as a process provides guidance and direction rather than definitive 'answers'.

There are still differing views and practices in the Restorative Justice movement, but many proponents would agree that, although it developed out of practice, Restorative Justice is not limited to any particular practice but rather is defined by an underlying set of principles. Marshall (1999) describes these as:

- making room for the personal involvement of those chiefly concerned (particularly the offender and the victim, but also their families and communities);
- seeing crime problems in their social context;
- a forward-looking (or preventive) problem-solving orientation;
- flexibility of practice.

As it developed in the criminal justice system, Restorative Justice outlined, perhaps for the first time, a much clearer framework for repair or restoration, in which harm could be addressed but within a context where the needs of both the person harmed and the person responsible for the harm are the priorities. This is based on the idea that the damaged relationship could and should be repaired; and that the offending individual could be reintegrated for the good of that individual but also for the good of the community as a whole.

Wachtel (2005) has suggested that this relational approach can be made effective only when fair process is observed, and he refers to the 'social discipline window' (Figure 2.1), adapted from Glasser (1969) to show the importance of involving individuals in decisions that affect them directly, and the central importance of working *with* them, rather than doing things *to* or *for* them. In this social discipline window, the vertical axis refers to the

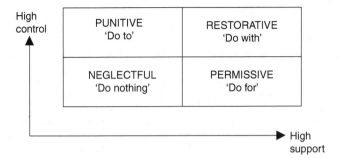

Figure 2.1 The social discipline window

Source: Adapted from Wachtel (2005) after Glasser (1969).

level of control exerted by those managing the process, while the horizontal axis refers to the level of support provided by those managing the process. High control and low support responses are referred to as 'punitive', authoritarian or retributive. High support without control is described as 'permissive', while low control and low support is 'neglectful'. (These ideas will be explored in more detail in Chapter 3.) According to Blood and Thorsborne, 'practice which maintains high standards and boundaries at the same time as being supportive is experienced as firm and fair (i.e. Restorative – the top right-hand box; working *with* others)' (2005, p. 10).

What is Restorative Justice and what does it look like?

During the past thirty years, three main Restorative Justice models have developed internationally. They are:

- mediation;
- circles;
- Restorative Justice conferences.

Practices associated with each of these models will now be outlined.

Mediation

Essentially, mediation is a process whereby a neutral third party (a specially trained mediator) supports those in conflict in coming to a mutually acceptable solution. Historically, there are three types of mediation models: community mediation, victim–offender reconciliation programmes (VORPs) and victim–offender mediation (VOM).

Mediation is not always considered to be an element of Restorative Justice. In some countries, including the United Kingdom, Mediation and Restorative

Justice have evolved into distinctive processes (see Chapter 5). However, most key understandings of Restorative Justice internationally borrow from mediation theory and practice (McCold and Wachtel 2003; Walgrave 2003). Howard Zehr's influential theory developed out of mediation practice, specifically VORPs, focusing on the interaction between victim and offender.

The standard process for community mediation was established in the early 1970s by the Institute for Mediation and Conflict Resolution (IMCR) in Manhattan, prior to any theoretical work on Restorative Justice (McGillis 1997). This followed the following framework, adapted from McCold (1996).

1 The mediator establishes ground rules.
2 The mediator makes a notification of confidentiality.
3 The mediator describes the consequences if the mediation fails – a return to court.
4 The parties give their versions of the dispute without interruption.
5 The parties participate in general discussion.
6 The mediator encourages the parties to make an agreement about their future conduct to each other.

Community mediation has its roots in civil dispute resolution; it is intended to divert disputes from going to litigation. In criminal cases the objective is to secure a written restitution agreement.

Circles

Models of Restorative Justice have often developed in response to demands from indigenous communities, for example in Canada and New Zealand, to make use of their own traditional approaches to conflict resolution. One example is given in the box that follows.

Work involving circles has also been developed strongly in the United Kingdom, both in schools and in the community. In schools there has been a huge expansion of 'circle time' (Moseley 2003) (Circle work in schools will be addressed in Chapter 5 of this book.) In social work, youth work and mental health fields the use of groupwork and counselling groups, based on circle work, developed as an important feature of practice in the 1980s and 1990s (Dwivedi 1993; Douglas 2000; Munn et al. 2000).

Healing circles

One of the best-known uses of circles is the Hollow Water First Nations Community Holistic Healing Circle. Initially, community members used circles to deal with the high level of alcoholism in

Hollow Water. In the safety of those circles, many began to disclose experiences of sexual abuse. This led to the development of healing circles as a way of dealing with the harm created by the offender, of healing the victim and restoring the community. The complete process involves thirteen stages: disclosure; establishing safety for the victim; confronting the offender; supporting the spouse/parent/child; supporting the extended family/community; meeting of the assessment team; circles with the offender; circles with the victim; circles with the offender's family; circles with the victim's family; sentencing circles to recommend disposition; sentencing review circles with the community; a cleansing circle.

Restorative Justice conferences

When used in criminal justice, a conference takes place in cases where offenders are accepting responsibility for their offence. They are asked to explain what happened, how they felt and what they think should be done to repair the harm done. The victims and others affected are asked to describe the physical, financial and emotional consequences of the crime and to identify what reparation might help. A plan of action is developed, and the goals of the conference are to encourage offenders to achieve empathy with their victims and take responsibility for their crimes, allowing victims to move towards forgiveness and healing (McCold 1996; Moore and O'Connell 1994). The legal systems in many countries now offer Restorative Justice conferencing to offenders and the person affected by a crime in an effort to bring the offender to a better understanding of the consequences of their actions on the person or persons involved. During this process the conference facilitator will follow a framework or 'script', using the following types of questions:

- What happened?
- What were you thinking at the time?
- What have you thought about since?
- Who has been affected by what you did?
- In what way?
- What do you think you need to do to put things right?

These questions are asked of the person responsible, while the person harmed has an opportunity to:

- say how they have been affected;
- ask questions of the person responsible;
- say what they need to happen to help put things right.

This would normally result in some form of action plan, with the Restorative Justice worker helping to ensure that this plan is followed through.

In the UK adult justice system, this type of conference has not taken the place of any punishment imposed by the courts but sits alongside it, with participants involved voluntarily in the process. In Scotland and other parts of the United Kingdom, children and young people involved in offending behaviour may be offered a Restorative Justice intervention as a diversion from other formal proceedings. The case study that follows illustrates how this process works in practice. This is a real example based closely on the notes of the youth justice worker involved in the case. Names and some details have been changed to maintain anonymity.

Restorative youth justice: example

Peter (13) and David (14) were referred to the Youth Justice Service for stealing a car from the car park at their school. The youth justice worker visited both boys individually. Each accepted responsibility for the incident and both said that they would be willing to meet the person harmed in a Restorative Meeting. During this preparatory work it became clear that there had been a significant time gap between the offence and the charge being brought by the police, and both boys said this uncertainty had caused them a great degree of anxiety.

Both boys engaged well with the Service worker and spoke openly and honestly about their part in the incident. The boys elected to go to the Restorative Conference on their own, without other support persons (e.g. parents).

Mr and Mrs Brown were the owners of the car. When the car was stolen, Mr Brown had been working as a teacher in the boys' school. The youth justice worker visited the couple in their home. They talked about what happened on the day of the incident and the effect it had had. Mrs Brown had been very ill at the time, so the inconvenience was great. Additionally, Mr Brown was concerned that it had been a personal attack by pupils who did not like him. They said that they were willing to meet with the two boys separately.

On both days of the meetings, Mrs Brown was not well enough to attend, so Mr Brown went to the meeting alone. The meetings gave both boys and Mr Brown the chance to discuss the incident and the impact and consequences for all involved. In both meetings the boys spoke frankly about their individual involvements, taking full responsibility for their actions. Through these meetings the boys heard from Mr Brown that Mrs Brown was unwell and that being without a car had caused the couple a lot of difficulties in getting on with their daily lives.

David told Mr Brown that at the time they took the car it had been very much an opportunist offence and they had no idea who the owner was. However, in the time between the theft and the boys being charged, one of David's friends, unaware of his involvement, had mentioned to David that Mr Brown's car had been stolen. His friend had indicated that this was really bad as Mr Brown was a good and well-liked teacher. David agreed with this sentiment and told Mr Brown this. This helped to allay Mr Brown's concerns that the theft was a result of personal grudges.

Both boys made sincere apologies and also asked that these be passed on to Mrs Brown. There was discussion about a possible reparative task. At Mr Brown's suggestion, both boys willingly undertook a piece of work with a local health charity. Mr Brown thanked both the boys for being so honest and wished them well for the future. He said that because of how the boys had responded to the incident they could be proud of themselves and told them they could 'hold their heads up' and should speak to him if ever they encountered him again.

How have the ideas of Restorative Justice evolved in schools?

Over time, some of those working in education, concerned about rising indiscipline and disaffection, began to ask whether a restorative approach might work in schools too. Others, who saw the role of school as central to making society as a whole more Restorative and just, joined them (Morrison 2007).

Over the past twenty-five years or so, education practitioners and other professionals in a variety of countries have adopted and adapted the approaches described above to suit school contexts. This had led to a range of interventions being developed, based on theoretical perspectives and practical frameworks derived from Mediation, Circles and Restorative Justice Conferences.

In a school context it is rarely appropriate to talk about 'offenders' and 'victims'; life is more complicated than that. The complex dynamics of school relationships mean that incidences of conflict and harm sometimes cannot be considered simply in terms of one individual's behaviour towards another. This is true both in the classroom and at breaks and lunchtimes. Schools are communities; most people know each other and meet on a daily basis. The adults and children who have to manage these difficulties in schools generally have ongoing relationships with each other. The underlying dynamics of incidents in schools and the need to repair and maintain ongoing relations have led to schools evolving a wide range of proactive and responsive Restorative Approaches (see Chapter 5 and 6).

The main ideas behind Restorative Practice in schools are that:

- The school system is the central institution in the development and education of all its citizens. This is reflected, for example, in the four purposes of the Scottish Curriculum for Excellence.
- Personal responsibility is most likely to flourish when there is genuine opportunity to participate in communal life.
- Daily interactions between staff themselves, between teacher and child, and between child and child have a cumulative effect on personal and social development.
- Good relationships within schools have a positive impact on learning outcomes.

These ideas or principles have led to Restorative Practice developments in schools across the world. Some examples follow.

The United States

Restorative Practice in schools in the United States developed first in work with troubled and troublesome children. One key school leader speaks of

> increasing truancy and dropout rates, disciplinary problems, violence, and even mass murders.... We believe that the dramatic increase in negative behavior among young people is largely the result of the loss of connectedness and community in modern society. Schools themselves have become larger, more impersonal.... In an increasingly disconnected world, restorative practice builds relationships and restores community.
>
> (Wachtel, 2004, p. 2)

He goes on to add:

> Restorative practices are about doing things *with* students, rather than *to* them or *for* them. Restorative practices hold young people accountable for their behavior, but in a way that is supportive and respectful, not punitive or demeaning.... Our approach is a method for changing the culture in a school in a deliberate, creative way.
>
> (Wachtel 2004, p. 2)

Schools have also used proactive circles, which might take the form of daily or weekly 'check-in' and 'check-out' circles in which each student answers a question in relation to an activity, goal or feeling. Teachers can also use this format responsively to address problematic incidents in class.

Australia

The initial use of Restorative Practice in Queensland schools in 1994 was in response to a serious assault after a school dance. Conferencing was later successfully introduced in New South Wales in 1997 as part of the Department of Education's Alternative to Suspension project. Examples of a more proactive approach in Australia were encouraging, and the introduction of an intervention programme (the Responsible Citizenship Programme) to prevent bullying and create a safe environment appeared to be beneficial. An evaluation in one primary school revealed that it created a shift in the way students interacted with one another in terms of respect, consideration and participation (Morrison 2002).

There have been similar commitments to the development of Restorative Practice in schools in Canada, New Zealand, Belgium, Hungary and the Netherlands.

The United Kingdom

In the United Kingdom, commitment to Restorative Practice is now developing strongly in some areas. Initiatives and developments to existing approaches to make them more restorative include:

- Restorative ethos building;
- Restorative language and scripts;
- Restorative Enquiry;
- Restorative Conversations;
- circles;
- mediation, including peer mediation and shuttle mediation;
- Restorative meetings, informal conferences, classroom conferences and mini-conferences;
- Restorative Conferencing;
- training in conflict resolution skills;
- curriculum focus on relationship building and conflict prevention and resolution;
- focus on citizenship (e.g. communication skills, anger management and the notion of responsibility).

What has been learned so far?

The ideas of Restorative Justice have been very attractive to schools, especially in the light of continuing concerns about behaviour and disengagement from schooling. Wachtel (2005, p. 1) talks about the need to restore 'community in a disconnected world' and says that the 'increasingly difficult and violent behavior among school students and related punitive school climate are both products of the alienation and loss of community that plagues modern society in general'. Against a background of high disciplinary exclusions in the United Kingdom and internationally, and as staff stress also continues to rise (Kelly and Colquhoun 2005; Munn *et al.* 2004), Restorative Practice offer a means of improving the experience of school for children, staff and parents alike.

Restorative Approaches have taken diverse forms in schools, and in this section we consider these further before reflecting on issues that arise through their implementation. The impact of Restorative Approaches can be gauged from evaluation studies (Cameron and Thorsborne 2001; Kane *et al.* 2007; Marsh and Crowe 1998; McGrath 2004; Smith and Hennessy 1999; Bitel 2005). Finally, in this chapter, we will consider the ways in which Restorative Approaches might further develop in schools.

Restorative Approaches have sometimes been described as existing on a continuum, with specific Restorative Justice techniques such as formal conferencing at one end of the spectrum and a range of related and permeating approaches such as peer mediation and circle time at the other end. Various approaches taken by schools may be located at different points on this continuum (see Chapter 5). Evaluation studies convey the diversity of these approaches. Some studies focus on Restorative Justice approaches towards children and young people in difficulty in school settings. Other studies consider Restorative Practice as providing a platform for the development of school ethos.

In England and Wales, the Youth Justice Board reported on a pilot initiative in which youth offending teams worked with twenty-six schools in England and Wales. The aims of the initiative were to reduce offending, bullying and victimization and to improve attendance, largely through conferencing. The evaluation concluded that Restorative Justice, while '*not a panacea for problems in schools*', could '*if implemented correctly... improve the school environment, enhance learning and encourage young people to become more responsible and empathetic*' (Bitel 2005, p. 13). There was also evidence that some of the key principles and practices of Restorative Justice were helpful in addressing issues of discipline in schools. These ways of implementing Restorative Practice, however, had little impact on outcome measures such as exclusions and no real improvement on child attitudes except in the small number of schools where a whole-school approach had been adopted.

Studies in Australia and New Zealand echo these findings (Blood and Thorsborne 2005; Drewery 2004; Porter 2005). A focus on conferencing was found to work well for wrongdoers and those harmed, but conferencing on its own was hard to sustain for schools, and had little impact on school cultures. However, when it was accompanied by a 'reculturing' of the whole school towards restorative principles, the impact of conferencing was optimized. A study by Preston (2002) of Restorative Practice initiatives in Buckingham and Oxfordshire lends further support to a twin-track approach to the implementation of Restorative Approaches in schools. She advocates that schools should think about Restorative Approaches as operating on two levels: preventive and restorative.

The most extensive study in the United Kingdom to date (Kane *et al.* 2007) was based on a two-year pilot involving eighteen Scottish schools in the primary, secondary and special education sectors. This research found that primary schools often emphasized whole-school, preventive approaches focusing on ethos, language and values in addition to curricular developments and particular practices such as Mediation, problem solving and Restorative Meetings. Mediation, shuttle mediation and peer mediation were widely used in primary schools in this study, whereas, at the other end of the continuum of approaches, Restorative Conferences were not a significant feature. Secondary schools were more likely to begin with one part of the school or with more challenging children and to develop Restorative Meetings, informal conferences and mediation. While formal conferencing was more in evidence than in primary schools, it was still not widely used. Some secondary schools developed wider approaches, spreading to subject departments and classrooms and revising their disciplinary and pastoral care processes along restorative lines. This study also noted a developing focus on the well-being of all children through Restorative Practice, rather than only on challenging behaviour and disengagement. Overall in the schools in this study, most energy went into developing child-focused Restorative Practice, although it was recognized that this also offered a means of conflict resolution among staff. Similarly, the involvement of parents, though recognized as desirable, was at an early stage of development in most schools.

What assisted the implementation of Restorative Approaches in schools and helped ensure their effectiveness?

Effective development of Restorative Approaches was seen to proceed from different starting points, with some opting for whole-school development and others using more focused strategies. No one model of effective implementation has emerged, but it is possible to identify a number of common features in schools that have successfully implemented Restorative Approaches:

- Schools getting the most out of Restorative Approaches were well positioned to start their implementation because they had already committed themselves to improving school ethos through related initiatives such as circle time.
- Primary schools in particular, though not exclusively, recognized the importance of establishing a network of positive relationships across

the school and in extending those relationships beyond the school and into the community. Restorative Approaches were seen to provide a vehicle for achieving this.

- Predictably, leadership played a vital role in the successful implementation of Restorative Approaches. Visible support and modelling of a Restorative Approach by senior managers and key child support staff helped to ensure that Restorative Approaches became embedded in school practices.

- Schools valued the flexibility to pursue Restorative Approaches in ways appropriate to the individual school. This resulted in diverse practices but also ensured that schools felt ownership of the implementation.

- Finally, from this evaluation it was clear that high-quality training and staff development were key to effective implementation, with opportunities for both school-based and external training being valued. Staff development led by school staff endorsed the idea of clear leadership and school ownership of the implementation process.

The introduction of Restorative Approaches also revealed tension with existing, more punitive discipline approaches:

> Our efforts to graft restorative practices on to a system which is basically punitive have proved frustrating, to say the least. But commendation is due here to those schools which, despite these overwhelming pressures to suspend and exclude difficult students, have grasped the nettle and recognised the contributions that restorative practices can make.
> (Cameron and Thorsborne 2001, p. 188)

In the Scottish evaluation too, and especially in secondary schools, the relationship between Restorative Approaches and established school discipline systems could be fraught with tensions. Those difficulties were not experienced most acutely in relation to exclusions. Schools reported that Restorative Approaches could be helpful in reaching a resolution that included formal exclusion processes. But existing whole-school 'behaviour management' systems based on essentially behavioural approaches, such as assertive discipline, could be experienced as conflicting with Restorative Practice principles of personal responsibility, the right to be heard and empathy between individuals involved (See Chapter 8 for a more detailed exploration of this topic.)

In the United Kingdom and further afield, evaluation studies of Restorative Approaches have yielded enough evidence of positive impact to demonstrate their value and to ensure that schools will go on refining and developing their approaches.

Future development trends

Schools participating in the Scottish evaluation (Kane *et al.* 2007) were seen to change their practices as they became more familiar with the ideas and values underpinning Restorative Approaches. It is possible to note trends in those changes, pointing the way forward for Restorative Approaches in schools.

1   Tensions revealed between existing philosophies and practices for managing behaviour and Restorative Practice, such as conferencing, became very pointed for some schools and led those schools to question well-established and punishment-based discipline policies. The *will to punish* (Parsons 2005) runs deep in schools and a shift away from that and towards preventive and Restorative ways of working will, for some schools, be slow and difficult but there are already examples of schools that have made significant progress in that process of culture change. (See the discssion of sanctions and rule-breaking in Chapter 4).

2   Conferencing will continue to play a small but significant role, while Restorative ethos building and preventive work will become increasingly central to schools' implementation. In that respect, secondary schools will be more likely to follow the 'whole-school' model of implementation prevailing in primary schools.

3   Many education services organize their pre-five, primary, secondary and special schools provision in local 'cluster' groups for management and development purposes. Such organizational arrangements will assist in the continuation of Restorative Approaches from the primary into the secondary sector.

4   Children themselves, if allowed, can be key to ethos-building initiatives in secondary schools. For example, children transferring from primary into S1 will have well-developed mediation skills and a wealth of experience in applying those skills, as a result of considerable investment by their primary schools. A challenge for secondary schools will be to recognize and to utilize the Restorative attitudes and skills already in the possession of incoming S1 children.

5   The role of parents and community will become increasingly important. As word about aspects of Restorative Practice spreads, schools identify a need to involve parents in workshops, allowing them to understand, and to cultivate, the attitudes, understandings and skills fostered by the school in the implementation of Restorative Practice. The changes in attitudes and behaviours in schools where Restorative Approaches have been successfully introduced are unlikely to become embedded in the culture of their communities without the understanding and active involvement of those communities.

Chapter 3

What is Restorative Practice in schools?

Restorative Practice in an educational context has been defined as 'restoring good relationships when there has been conflict or harm; and, developing school ethos, policies and procedures to reduce the possibility of such conflict and harm arising'.
(Restorative Practices in three local authorities: Evaluation of pilot projects 2004–2006, Scottish Executive, 2007)

This chapter covers:

Relationships at the core of learning
Why relationships matter
Restorative values
Restorative attitudes
Skills for Restorative Approaches
Restorative Processes: the role of the school
Teaching: proactive approaches to pro-social learning
Modelling: the way we are with others
Intervening: responsive approaches to incidents of conflict and harm
A whole-school approach to relationships

Relationships at the core of learning

Restorative Practice provides a particular philosophical approach to the relational aspects of working together. Restorative Practice in schools is fundamentally about the building, maintaining and repairing of relationships. This approach recognizes that relationships among those in the school community – between teachers and learners, between learners themselves, between colleagues and between staff and parents – have a profound influence on learning. To understand the basis of this approach, we need first to understand why it is that relationships are so centrally important to children's learning and well-being.

What do we mean by 'relationships' in this context?

You cannot work in a school and avoid relationships; relationships are inevitable. In the broadest sense, as soon as you start communicating verbally with someone (and sometimes before you start), you begin to create a relationship – by which we mean the developing perceptions and understandings that individuals have of each other and how these are communicated. Each relationship in a school, however apparently shallow or deep, is unique and dynamic and so is susceptible to influence – and therein lies the potential for change, individual learning and growth. A belief in *every* individual's capacity for this learning and growth is fundamental to Restorative Practice.

Why relationships matter

Of course, the relationships that we have in schools are not the be-all and end-all of the learning and teaching process. As a teacher, you have varying degrees of control over a range of important factors, including your relationships, all of which can influence the quality of the work you do and the quality of the learner's experience. Some of the key factors are summarized in Table 3.1.

The importance of the factors in the first three rows (time available, the curriculum and resources) is self-evident and cannot be ignored. For instance, if you do not engage your learners in relevant, challenging or enjoyable learning, then the quality of your relationships with them is of limited value in terms of their learning. However, the day-to-day pressures and constraints associated with managing time, the curriculum and resources can at times divert our attention from the relational factors that are within our influence – that is, the individual relationships we experience on a daily basis. At other times, individual relationships may be to the fore, perhaps because they are particularly rewarding or particularly stressful. But the reality is that these relationships surround us constantly.

Indeed, there are so many relationships in a teacher's daily life that sometimes it is easier to think of groups of people as single entities – 'What a lovely class!' or 'Not that bunch again!' For example, if you start working with a class of twenty students, you will be creating in your own mind

Table 3.1 Factors that influence learning

As a teacher I have less control over:	As a teacher I have more control over:
The time available to me	How I use this time
What I have to teach (the curriculum)	How I teach (my methodology)
Resources available to support learning	How I use these resources
The learners I am given to teach	The relationships I build with them
The colleagues I have to work with	The relationships I build with them
The parents/carers I have to work with	The relationships I build with them

unique perceptions of those twenty individuals. Each student, in turn will be forming a perception of you. In all, that is forty different sets of personal perceptions, each directly involving you. You have the greatest influence over twenty of these perceptions (your perception of each student) and you can strongly influence twenty more (their perceptions of you).

It doesn't stop there, though. Within this group of twenty-one people (including you) there are potentially 210 one-to-one relationships. That is 420 sets of individual perceptions – and you potentially have some influence over all of these. And that is without considering all your relationships with your colleagues and parents. However limited some of these relationships may be, there is no denying that, numerically at least, relationships in schools are a big issue.

Relationships of course involve far more than a science of numbers. Reflecting on your own experience of the teacher–learner relationship may help to clarify this issue.

Reflections

Remember a particular teacher who positively influenced your learning and development when you were a child at school. They may have used excellent teaching methodologies or been very effective in their use of resources, but, chances are, you remember particular personal qualities that made a difference to you and consequently to your attitude to learning. It may have been their sense of humour, their directness and honesty, their ability to accept you as a person, their faith in your ability or some other aspect that made you feel valued and that you, in turn, valued in them.

Think of a group of learners that you currently work with. With which learner(s) do you interact most effectively and with which least effectively? Pick two or three in each category and think about how they engage with their learning. Check out whether there is any link between those learners with whom you have less effective relationships and the quality of their engagement in learning in your class.

> *Surely it's a 'chicken and egg' situation, though. I find it harder to relate positively with those children who don't want to engage with their learning, or with those who won't meet my expectations.*

If it is indeed a 'chicken and egg' dilemma, then you cannot be sure which comes first. What you can be sure of is that you cannot *control* a child's attitude to learning.

- Might their relationship with you have an impact on their attitude to learning?
- How might you test out this hypothesis?
- Do you have a professional responsibility to consider how you might influence this relationship for the better?

Surely people can learn even in the absence of positive relationships?

Of course they can. People can learn through many media where relationships are not an obvious component part of the learning experience. Put a young child in a room with a number of new and interesting objects, and no other people, and they will not take long to start exploring and learning from their new surroundings. Give an older child access to the Internet and they can learn a great deal without relating to anyone else. The presence of an effective relationship does not appear to be necessary for any one individual learning event.

But many of the skills and cognitive processes that a child uses to explore and learn within these environments will have been developed as a result of interactions with significant people throughout their life. Furthermore, we know how much more quickly a child can learn a new concept or skill when the learning experience is supported or scaffolded by a skilled person. This, after all, is why we provide children with teachers!

We know that children engage in important learning in groups and can learn quickly from each other. What parent would see it as ideal to have their child educated entirely in isolation from others? We also know that when a child has been exposed to prolonged negative relationships with their caregivers, there is usually a negative impact on their ability to learn.

Humans are genetically programmed to be social learners. Effective communication with those around us is the primary conduit for our learning, not only in terms of curricular learning but, more importantly, in terms of learning about ourselves – our self-concept development. Restorative Practice aims to establish (or re-establish) constructive communication through the application of a particular set of values, attitudes, skills and processes.

Restorative values

Restorative Practice encompasses a wide range of ways of working, all of which share a common set of values. These include:

- respecting individuals' rights;
- taking responsibility for our own behaviour;

- believing that people can change;
- being open to supporting others who wish to change their behaviours;
- believing that Restorative responses are more helpful than retributive ones. (See the next section for an explanation of this distinction.)

Underpinning these values is the belief that Restorative Practice can be used effectively only when people become involved voluntarily in the process. Because of this, establishing a climate in which people actively participate and are willing to take part is one of the key challenges for Restorative practitioners. How effectively we engage with others will depend on the range of attitudes that we demonstrate in working together.

Restorative attitudes

How we choose to work with people reflects our attitudes to those individuals, as well as reflecting our beliefs about people in general. In Chapter 2 I introduced McCold and Watchel's description of four distinctive attitudinal perspectives when working with people: neglectful, permissive, retributive and restorative. They define these in terms of:

- the level of control (high or low) exercised by the adults in managing any process or intervention;
- the level of support (high or low) offered by the adults to those all those affected by the problem situation.

Figure 3.1 is an adapted summary of these perspectives.

A *neglectful* attitude is characterized by low control and low support. There is a tendency to ignore or not act on any concerns, despite being aware of them. 'Tactical ignoring' of certain low-level disturbing or inappropriate behaviours can be an effective strategy in some contexts. However, it is clearly not to be recommended as a general approach to all concerns!

A *permissive* attitude is characterized by low control and high support. There is a tendency to act on behalf of, and consequently to take responsibility away from, others. This is typified by apparently supportive interventions that actually deskill or disempower the individuals concerned. It may also involve making excuses for certain actions or behaviours while not acknowledging the impact of those behaviours on others.

A *retributive* attitude is characterized by high control and low support. There is a tendency to 'do to' others, without actively engaging them in any process. This way of thinking can be driven by a need for revenge. It can be driven by the belief that punishing wrongdoers will change their behaviour for the better. It can be driven by the belief that punishment for some will deter others from behaving in similar ways. A retributive

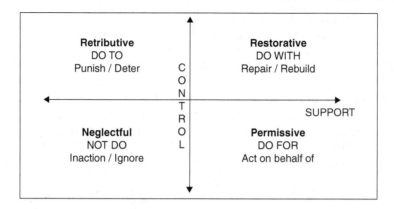

Figure 3.1 Attitudinal perspectives

Source: Adapted from Wachtel (2005) after Glasser (1969).

response may also be driven by the need for an authority figure to be seen to be 'doing something', in order to avoid potential criticism for being either neglectful or permissive. School responses that are sanctions based are essentially retributive, regardless of the degree to which these sanctions are 'counterbalanced' by the availability of formalized rewards or praise systems. When a child is subjected to a sanction, the knowledge that there are concrete rewards available for more acceptable behaviours does not make the experience of the sanction any more positive or purposeful for that child.

A *restorative* attitude is characterized by high control and high support. There is a tendency to engage fully with others in addressing concerns. All those involved will have opportunities to contribute to the restorative process, which will be managed by a skilled practitioner. The aim here is to meet the needs of all concerned while openly and constructively addressing any issues of conflict, harm and wrongdoing.

The box that follows provides an illustration of how these attitudes might be demonstrated in different responses to a particular problem.

There is of course a danger in characterizing attitudes in such bald terms. Labelling a person, or for that matter a school, as neglectful, permissive, retributive or restorative is generally going to be unhelpful. The reality is that most of us are capable of demonstrating a range of these attitudes and behaviours, depending on individual circumstances, our feelings at the time, and so on. However, these distinctions can be useful if they help us to describe particular attitudes and behaviours and so help us to focus on how we can shift towards more restorative ways of working, either in our own practice or in the wider approaches that our school adopts.

A range of attitudes

Mary complains to her teacher that John has been unkind to her in the playground. She says he is calling her unpleasant names and teasing her about her hair. His teacher, knowing John is a difficult pupil to work with, tells Mary that John is just trying to get her attention. She advises Mary to ignore the name-calling and teasing, and tells her that he will give up doing it after a while if she stops reacting to him.

This is essentially a neglectful response.

The next day, Mary's father phones the headteacher of the school. He is very angry that Mary is being treated in this way and that the school seems to be doing nothing about it. He demands that John be excluded from school for bullying.

This is a retributive response.

The headteacher, aware that there may be difficulties in John's home, phones his mother and asks her to come in to discuss the concern. John's mother argues that his behaviour is understandable as he is having a difficult time adjusting to a new stepfather in the house. She promises to have a word with John and asks the school to be understanding and to take no further action on this occasion.

This is a permissive response.

Instead, the headteacher gets the agreement of both parents and children to bring them together in a Restorative Meeting. The headteacher uses this process to help John to better understand the consequences of his behaviour towards Mary and take responsibility for it. Mary has an opportunity to say how she has been affected by John's behaviour, and agreement is reached on how John could put things right now and how his future behaviour will be different. This process includes John making an apology to Mary.

This is a restorative response.

Reflection: Think back over the past week and try to identify at least one time when each of the above attitudes influenced how you felt, thought or acted, either because you or someone else demonstrated that attitude.

The range of practical options available to us at any one time will influence how we choose to respond to any given difficulty. Undoubtedly individuals and schools sometimes make a neglectful, permissive or retributive response not because they feel this is the most appropriate response in the context, but simply because they do not fully understand the potential benefits of a restorative response or do not have the knowledge and skills to offer it. This was certainly the case in most UK schools twenty years ago. However, as knowledge, expertise, and evidence of the effectiveness of Restorative Practice have increased in recent years, the argument that there is no effective alternative no longer serves as an adequate excuse for inadequate responses.

In order to translate restorative attitudes into effective Restorative Practice, we need to be able to call on a range of relevant skills.

Skills for Restorative Approaches

The effective use of any Restorative Approach requires the practitioner to have a range of interpersonal skills, including the ability to:

- be an active listener;
- communicate empathically;
- communicate assertively;
- reflect on the consequences for others of one's own behaviour;
- understand and address the consequences of others' behaviours;
- manage interpersonal processes with consistency.

These skills are not unique to Restorative Approaches, and many staff in schools will already have developed these skills, albeit to varying degrees. Restorative Practice provides a particular framework in which we can make use of these skills, and appropriate development and training are essential if staff are to learn to use these skills to manage a range of restorative processes effectively. The issue of staff training will be considered in detail in Chapter 7.

Restorative processes: the role of the school

The complex dynamics that exist within schools provide opportunities for socially rich experiences for all learners. Children will learn from their relationships within schools whether we consciously choose to focus on these relationships, take them for granted or ignore them. If we accept this central role for relationships in young people's learning, then schools that ignore the issue of relationships do so to the likely detriment of their learners.

In Chapter 1 we considered the 'curriculum, modelling and intervening' model when considering relationships in schools. Restorative Practice provides a framework for working within each of these three aspects.

Teaching: proactive approaches to pro-social learning

I have argued that children will always learn something from the relationships that they experience at school. So, it makes sense for schools to focus explicitly on how they *teach* children about socializing – about their social awareness and their interpersonal skills. There is now good research evidence (Durlak *et al.* 2008) that learners who are offered such proactive approaches (that is, school-based curricular programmes that focus on social and emotional learning) benefit from the experience in a number of ways. Compared to students who do not receive this kind of learning, students offered such programmes improve significantly with respect to:

- social and emotional skills;
- attitudes about themselves, others and school;
- social and classroom behaviour;
- behaviour problems and aggression;
- conditions involving emotional distress, such as stress and depression;
- achievement in test scores and examination grades.

What is more, follow-up studies looking at each of the above categories have shown that these positive benefits to students persist over time.

We may view the teaching of emotional intelligence as a professional responsibility. Alternatively, we may view it as simply a normal and necessary part of human interaction with children. Either way, the case for the inclusion of explicit social learning programmes for all children in schools is now compelling.

Chapter 5 will take a closer look at the thinking and practice behind these types of Proactive Approaches.

Modelling: the way we are with others

Children are perceptive observers of adults. The way in which we relate to and respond to them provides a model for their future behaviours. Their observing is not necessarily a conscious effort; we are all capable of 'absorbing' the influence of another person into our own behaviours without necessarily considering explicitly what we are observing or experiencing. This is especially true for children and young people. The process of learning from adult modelling starts first with the baby's experience, then the infant's experience of being parented, but continues significantly for every child into school life.

When a child observes adults and learns from their attitudes or behaviours, there are three possible outcomes. The child can:

1   assimilate similar attitudes and behaviours;
2   choose *not* to behave in similar ways;
3   remain relatively uninfluenced by the adult's behaviour.

Which path the child takes will depend on how the child feels about that adult – in other words, on the nature of the relationship between the adult and the child, *as perceived by the child*. Modelling is a potentially significant way of influencing children's attitudes and behaviours, and will be most influential in a positive way when the child trusts, respects or admires the adult concerned.

If children in schools experience adults as people who communicate constructively, help to resolve conflict and address harm when it occurs, then we can increase the chances of their adopting similar attitudes and behaviours in their relationships with others. If, on the other hand, we choose to ignore this aspect of children's learning, leaving the outcomes to chance, then we neglect significant opportunities to help children equip themselves for the classroom, the playground and their experiences beyond the school gate. Being effective 'models' requires the adults in a school to practise what they preach.

> If we are not modelling what we teach, then we are teaching something else.
>
> (Helen Flanagan)

For example, where we expect children to respect adults and each other, then we need to be explicit in modelling respect for all the children and adults with whom we work. This is particularly important for those children who have little experience of being respected. It is often these children who find it hardest to demonstrate respect for others.

Behind this apparently simple idea lie some complex realities. Each member of staff will generally model a range of attitudes and behaviours in their interactions with children and adults. This diversity of staff approaches can be a strength in itself. However, while this range of experience can support children in understanding that we are each individuals, capable of a range of different responses in different contexts, some children can also find too much diversity or inconsistency in adult approaches confusing, and even disturbing. The challenge for any school implementing Restorative Practice is to strike a balance between promoting consistency in inter-personal approaches and respecting individuality.

> If a school aspires to be an inclusive community, then how tolerant should it be of a variety of adult attitudes and behaviours among its staff?

There is of course no simple answer to this question, but this is not a reason for avoiding it. Indeed, it is hard to see how a school could go down the path of implementing Restorative Practice without addressing this question with staff. If we are to achieve an effective balance between appropriate modelling and tolerance of individuality of teacher approach, any programme of implementation needs to consider the implications not only for individual staff but also for the school community as a whole. The philosophy and frameworks inherent in Restorative Practice provide a coherent approach to addressing these issues. The implications of modelling, as a way of working, will be considered in more detail in Chapter 7. Chapter 8 will consider the issue of consistency of approach among staff.

Intervening: responsive approaches to incidents of conflict and harm

All children can learn by observing the attitudes and behaviours of others. However, the more actively involved a child is in the process, the richer the learning experience. When we as adults intervene in situations involving conflict or harm, the way in which we choose to intervene may have a profound effect on those involved in the process, not only in terms of their experience at the time, but also for their longer-term learning.

Restorative Approaches offer a range of distinctive interventions that are specific to contexts of conflict or harm and that can be sensitively adapted to suit the level of concern and the tariff of the intervention. In recent years, two distinct types of intervention have developed in the wider field of Restorative Practice in the community. These interventions are often labelled as Mediation and Restorative Justice. Each has evolved to serve a particular purpose and to address particular types of concerns. Each of these intervention processes has subsequently been adopted and adapted in school contexts in a variety of ways.

The full range of Restorative interventions will be explored in more detail in Chapter 6.

A whole-school approach to relationships

In its broadest sense, then, Restorative Practice in schools is about establishing and, where necessary, repairing effective working relationships. Schools that implement Restorative Practice most effectively see this as a 'whole-school approach to relationships'. The proactive and responsive elements of Restorative Practice can be integrated into the day-to-day working of the school through the attitudes and behaviours of the staff (modelling), through planned learning opportunities embedded in the curriculum, and through the specific interventions that staff and pupils use when things go wrong between people. Figure 3.2 summarizes the key components of this whole-school approach.

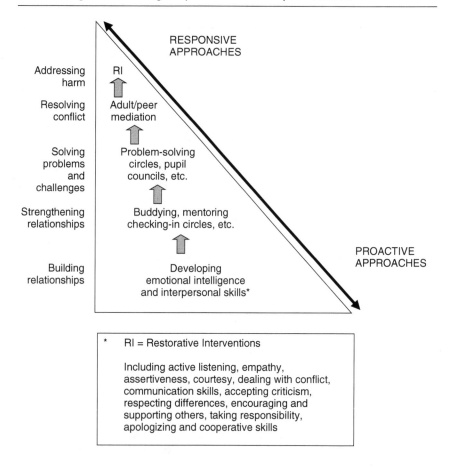

Figure 3.2 A whole-school approach to relationships

Source: Adapted from Brookes (2005).

Framed in this way, a number of considerations relating to such a whole-school approach become evident. First, to be successful, the bulk of our effort needs to be focused on building interpersonal skills and constructive relationships. The more effectively this is achieved, the fewer the incidents of conflict and harm that will arise. As a result, schools that have implemented this whole-school approach to Restorative Practice have reported a decrease over time in their reliance on sanctioned-based approaches. Conversely, if we choose to take a neglectful approach to the teaching of interpersonal skills and simply 'bolt on' Restorative Interventions as a reactive response when things go wrong, then we invite inconsistency and lack of cohesion in our practice.

Second, schools that have a graduated range of support systems and interventions will be best placed to respond to particular concerns at an appropriate level and will minimize the risks of either over-reacting or being neglectful.

Third, as Restorative Interventions always need to be voluntary in order to be effective, schools will need to have recourse to other processes for the small number of occasions when it proves impossible or inappropriate to use a Restorative Intervention.

Finally, the implementation of such an all-encompassing approach to relationships and schools is clearly no small task. School communities, as much as individual staff, need to consider how ready they are to implement Restorative Practice and to plan the pace of change within their usual planning frameworks. Experience suggests that for most schools this is likely to involve a two- to five-year development programme. In considering such a significant commitment, schools need to weigh up whether the benefits merit the level of effort required.

This whole-school approach to relationships allows schools to focus consciously and consistently on issues of respect, social responsibility, self-regulation and effective support. The potential benefits in terms of improved socialization, motivation, attainment and ethos have already been realized in many schools across the world.

In Chapter 4 we will consider how Restorative Practice sits with the retributive responses which many schools still feel they need to rely on in responding to incidences of conflict and harm.

The range of contexts for using Restorative Approaches

Constructive communication does not develop in schools by chance. We can choose how we respond to conflict. We should not ignore feelings of harm.

This chapter covers:

Establishing constructive communication
Resolving conflict
Addressing harm
Why shame matters
Acknowledging and addressing moral inequalities
Responding to harm, conflict and communication breakdown: which should come first?
What are your rules for?
How effective are your rules and sanctions?
Rule breaking and wrongdoing in a retributive culture
Rule breaking and wrongdoing in a restorative culture
Where do sanctions fit in?

Introduction

Schools are microcosms of their wider communities. They reflect the diversity of relationships and experiences that exist beyond the school gates, as well as offering contexts for relationships that are peculiar to the school setting. It would be unreasonable and also unrealistic to suggest that one single approach could serve as a template for addressing all the complexities and challenges that relationships in schools throw up on a daily basis.

One of the strengths of Restorative Practice is the range of approaches that it encompasses. Some of these approaches have already been introduced in Chapters 2 and 3. Table 4.1 lists those most commonly used at present in UK schools, separated broadly into proactive approaches and responsive interventions.

Table 4.1 Common Restorative Approaches in UK schools

Proactive approaches	Responsive interventions
Modelling	Problem-solving circles
Curriculum-based programmes in emotional intelligence	Peer (student) mediation
	Adult mediation
Community building and 'checking-in' circles	Restorative language and enquiry
Conflict resolution skills programmes	Restorative Conversations
Buddying or befriending	Restorative (face-to-face) Meetings
Mentoring	Restorative Conferences

Figure 4.1 shows how these approaches can be broadly classified not only on a proactive versus responsive spectrum, but also by their appropriateness in relation to the seriousness or 'tariff' of the concern.

There are of course other responsive interventions that would not be characterized as 'restorative'. These include support groups and circles, counselling, and cognitive behavioural and skills-based programmes, each of which has a potentially positive role to play in supporting individuals.

This range of approaches is potentially bewildering for any individual or school wishing to implement Restorative Practice. A more detailed exploration of some of these proactive approaches and responsive interventions forms the basis for Chapters 5 and 6 respectively. It may be helpful if we first explore the different purposes of these approaches and why they have arisen. This exploration is made easier if we can consider three distinctive aspects of relationships: *communication*, *conflict* and *harm*.

Establishing constructive communication

In this book I identify *constructive communication* as an important and central feature of Restorative Practice. By constructive communication I mean interpersonal communication (verbal and non-verbal) that is clear, honest, respectful and appropriately supportive. Constructive communication between individuals lies at the heart of meaningful learning and positive relationships. Where constructive communication exists in a school, the members of that community, including pupils and staff, will be using and developing a range of effective interpersonal skills and qualities. These include:

- *articulacy* – the ability to express and communicate our feelings, thoughts and needs;
- *assertiveness* – the ability to articulate these feelings, thoughts and needs in ways that neither diminish nor disrespect others or ourselves;
- *respect* – both for others and for ourselves;
- *empathy* – the process of striving to understand someone else's perspective.

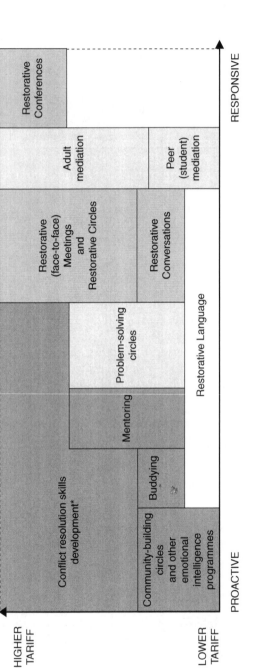

Figure 4.1 The range of Restorative Approaches in schools

Key

The **primary** focus is on building relashionships and/or on developing individual's capacities and skills.

The **primary** focus is on resolving problems and interpersonal conflict.

The **primary** focus is on addressing harm done with respect to both the person(s) responsible and the person(s) harmed.

* Conflict resolution skills can be offered across the proactive/responsive and high/low tariff spectra.

These skills and qualities are sometimes described collectively as 'emotional intelligence' or 'emotional literacy'. This book will use the former term.

Those who work in schools know the importance of establishing constructive communication with new pupils and classes, as well as with parents and colleagues. They also know the challenges that can arise when someone is lacking in some or all of the above skills. Ineffective communication, whether with students, parents or colleagues, is often the source of misunderstanding, misinterpretation and misrepresentation. Therefore, schools that wish to engage meaningfully with their learners will aim to *teach them* effective communication skills, rather than risk assuming that all children and young people will come through the school gate already skilled in constructive communication. This teaching of skills will be done both through curricular opportunities and through the modelling that staff provide. Staff themselves should have opportunities to develop their communication and interpersonal skills through continuing professional development. Facilitating constructive communication between people is an essential feature of all Restorative Approaches and responsive interventions.

In recent years a number of distinctive approaches have been developed which aim to support children in learning the interpersonal skills that lead to constructive communication. Chapter 5 will consider some current examples and also identify some of the shared features of these approaches.

Resolving conflict

'Conflict' is a broad term that is commonly used to describe anything from two children falling out in the playground to all-out war between nations. For the purposes of this book I wish to focus on the interpersonal aspects of conflict. In this respect, a conflict can be defined as an interpersonal process – a disagreement or clash between people based on their ideas, needs or beliefs. The ability to express these ideas, needs or beliefs is an essential part of being human. The ideas, needs or beliefs of one person will not always be in accord with those of others, and so conflict can arise whenever two or more people compete to assert their differing ideas, needs or beliefs. Conflict, in this sense, is therefore a normal part of human relationships.

It can be tempting to think that a school without conflict would be a delightful place in which to work and learn. However, if children were able to spend their formative years in a school where they experienced no conflict at all, we would have to consider what kind of preparation this would be for the conflict they would encounter in the wider world. Disagreements, arguments and falling out with friends are essential parts of social development and, because they are experienced so personally, are rich learning experiences for us all.

Importantly, conflict, in the sense of the word used here, generally implies a *moral equality* between disputants. People may hold fundamentally different views on a matter. They may or may not be able to reach a mutually accept-able compromise, solution or agreement to resolve their conflict. However, as long as one person is not imposing a solution on (or in some other way caus-ing harm to) the other person, then each holds their views from a position of moral equivalence.

When someone chooses to intervene to help resolve such a conflict from a restorative perspective, it is important that the process acknowledge this moral equality. The process offered should reflect the fact that the partici-pants have a shared responsibility for the conflict and should also recognize that each deserves to be given equal opportunity and responsibility for cre-ating a resolution. This moral balance shifts when one person has clearly harmed another, and this, in turn, has implications for the nature of inter-vention that is offered. The issue of harm and moral responsibility will be considered in more detail later in this chapter.

If children are going to learn effectively and develop personal resilience, then they will need to learn to manage and resolve the conflicts that they encounter on a day-to-day basis. Restorative Approaches have much to offer here:

- Proactive approaches focus on the teaching and modelling of effective conflict resolution skills through experiential learning activities that help pupils to link explicitly their thoughts and feelings to their behaviours.
- Responsive interventions to conflict resolution, such as Mediation, cre-ate an emotionally safe framework that helps people to resolve their own conflicts by seeking a 'win–win' solution (see Figure 4.2).

Mediation, as a specific type of intervention, will be considered in more detail in Chapter 6.

Addressing harm

'Harm' has been elaborated on as

> including harm which is not physical harm. This not only covers the deliberate infliction of physical or mental harm but also where harm resulted, or might have resulted, from a degree of carelessness or neglect that amounted to misconduct. There is no definitive list of types of behaviour that are considered harmful... this may depend on indi-vidual circumstances.
>
> (Adapted from the Protection of Children (Scotland) Act 2003)

Harm, then, can be seen as a personal outcome – something experienced and perceived by the individual. Harm often arises out of unresolved or escalat-ing conflict. But it can also arise where little or no conflict precedes it – for

Figure 4.2 A win–win solution

example in the case of an unprovoked theft or assault. While every experience of harm is in some respects unique, the experience of harm brings with it some predictable emotional responses:

- A person who has been harmed is likely to feel anxiety and stress regarding the incident as well as an ongoing feeling of hurt. They may worry about the possible recurrence of similar incidents in the future. They may also experience confusion about why they were harmed.
- A person responsible for harm may also experience confusion and stress about the incident. They may feel the need to justify their actions. They may regret what they have done, experience shame or feel remorse.

The experience of being harmed can obviously leave a person feeling vulnerable. However, the act of harming someone else may well have put the *person responsible for the harm* in a potentially vulnerable position as well – in the sense that they will have exposed themselves to possible rejection by the other person, their social group or the wider community. Where a person responsible for causing harm experiences this anxiety about rejection, or where they feel they have broken their own moral code of conduct, they will usually experience some form of *shame*.

It is not unusual for people who have been harmed to also report feelings of shame, however apparently illogical this may appear. Although their needs may appear quite different from those of the person responsible for the harm, they too have been placed in a vulnerable position and may be feeling isolated and unsupported.

From a restorative perspective, both the person harmed and the person responsible for the harm are of equal value. Both have needs and both should be offered an opportunity to play their part in any Restorative Intervention. A key part of this intervention will be to support those involved in managing any feelings of shame.

Why shame matters

Much work has been done in the field of criminal justice on the role of shame in helping offenders to face up to their wrongdoing and to reintegrate into their communities. Braithwaite (1989) has described why a consideration of shame is necessary if we are to allow people to take responsibility for their offending behaviours and to help them consider how they might adapt these behaviours in the future. However, 'shame' is not a word that we are necessarily comfortable with when considering children and young people in schools. This is perhaps because we associate the word 'shame' (a noun) with the word 'shaming' (a verb). 'Shaming' is often perceived as a deeply unpleasant process – something that is 'done to' others by those who wish to exert power over others in order to 'put them in their place', manipulate their behaviour or assert hierarchical authority.

> ### Reflection
> You may remember particularly poignant incidents when you were at school, involving yourself or others being 'shamed' in this way by teachers.

Shaming can also carry connotations of public humiliation and derision – as in the concept of 'naming and shaming'.

There is no doubt that our culture holds a rich vein of retributive associations with the idea of shame. This is reflected in the wide vocabulary that we have created that describes processes that attempt to 'induce' shame in others, for example *give someone a row, reprimand, correct, admonish, rebuke, chastise, impose a sanction, punish, etc.* However, this notion of shaming – a process that is 'done to' others – is clearly not compatible with restorative thinking. Culturally, our language is comparatively thin on terms that describe or explain less judgemental and more restorative experiences of shame. This perhaps helps explain why some of the terminology from the field of Restorative Practice can at first sound somewhat contrived.

From a restorative perspective, shame involves physiological and psychological processes that we can all experience when our actions or experiences have led us to feel socially vulnerable. In adopting this perspective on shame, it becomes apparent that any process that aims to address harm or wrongdoing directly with the individuals involved needs to take account of their individual feelings of shame. And so a grasp of how we can help people to manage shame is fundamental to developing our understanding of why a Restorative Intervention can be such a powerful way of addressing incidents of harm and wrongdoing.

There are certain physical and physiological signs that will often indicate that a person is feeling shame, even when that person does not consciously or overtly express these feelings. Typical signs of these include:

- drooping shoulders and head (lowered muscle tone, slouching);
- avoidance of eye contact (an unwillingness to 'look the person in the eye');
- lowered tone of voice (mumbling);
- dilation of superficial blood vessels (blushing or flushing).

An example of how these typical shame reactions can be misinterpreted and how this misinterpretation can adversely affect a discourse may be helpful here.

Shame reactions

As a young teacher I overheard a pupil swearing aggressively at another pupil in class. Shocked by his behaviour, I took the offending pupil out into the corridor and, in angry tones, asked what on earth he thought he was doing, talking like that in my class.

The pupil stood slouching against the wall, with his eyes downcast as he mumbled an inaudible response. This angered me further as I (mis)interpreted this behaviour as a sign of his defiance and unwillingness to accept that what he had done was wrong.

'Stand up straight and look at me properly when I'm talking to you!' I insisted. The boy reluctantly looked up at me. His face had now changed to express apparent resentment and anger. Things did not get better thereafter!

In my ignorance I had failed to understand that by responding in this way I had denied the pupil the opportunity to express appropriately his feelings of shame. Instead of working with the boy to help him manage his shame, to accept responsibility and then to move on to what he could and should do differently, I had made him the butt of my indignation. By trying to brow-beat him into feeling ashamed I had, in effect, compounded the breakdown in communication that had been initiated by his inappropriate behaviour. (An example of how a Restorative Conversation that might address this kind of incident more appropriately can be found in Chapter 6.)

Of course, the outward physical indicators of shame may be masked by more noticeable behaviours, particularly if the person feels the need to defend their actions or to deny their feelings of shame. Shame is not a pleasant experience and we can become skilled at hiding or denying our sense of shame, even to ourselves. As shame itself is a stressor, we can respond to feelings of shame through typical 'fight' or 'flight' reactions such as avoidance, blaming others or aggression towards others. These responses neatly divert our own attention, and that of others, away from our feelings of shame.

Brookes has characterized the range of fight and flight responses to shame using the diagram shown in Figure 4.3. Some of these reactions are commonplace, and recognizable in the behaviours of many pupils. Others, although more extreme, may nonetheless be linked to feelings of shame.

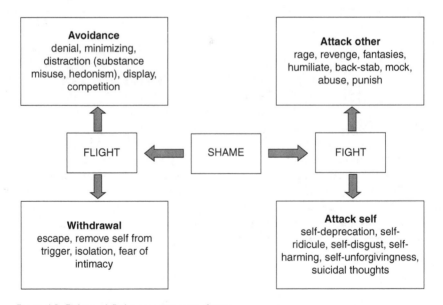

Figure 4.3 Fight and flight responses to shame

Source: Adapted by Brookes (2005) from Nathanson, (1992).

There is no simple way to predict what shame reactions an individual will express in any given situation, although patterns of reaction can become evident as we get to know individuals and their behaviours.

One purpose of a Restorative Intervention in this context is to help the person responsible for the harm to experience and manage their own feelings of shame. This experience of shame is often a necessary first step towards fully accepting responsibility for the impact of their behaviour on others. Consequently, a lack of regard for this fundamental aspect of the restorative process is likely to result in an unwillingness to apologize and make amends on the part of the person responsible (as in the example above). Or, where an apology is forthcoming, it is likely to feel forced, contrived or half-hearted. Chapter 6 explains how the skilful use of an appropriate Restorative Intervention can help the person responsible to make a *genuine* apology and reparation in ways that do not involve them in being inappropriately shamed or demeaned.

Acknowledging and addressing moral inequalities

Do schools have a responsibility to teach children the difference between 'right' and 'wrong'?

Although most schools would answer a clear 'Yes' to this question concerning moral education, this is a complex philosophical topic that could merit a book in itself. For example, whose moral code are we teaching? In some faith schools this may be a relatively straightforward question to answer, as the relevant faith will provide the moral guidance and framework for interpersonal conduct. Non-denominational schools will generally also have developed an explicit or implicit moral code that they wish to transmit to their learners, derived perhaps (though not necessarily) from the social values of the wider community. This moral code will generally be reflected in their school values, rules or codes of conduct. But, as teachers, to what degree do we want children to 'introject' (absorb uncritically) the moral code of others rather than to develop a moral code of their own, one that they will fully accept and act on? This philosophical question is too broad for the scope of this book.

Regardless of whether the school sees its role as 'handing on' an externally defined moral code or as helping each child to develop their own internal moral code, issues of wrongdoing and harm will still arise and need responding to. The school as an institution, and the staff in their role as its representatives, will need to make judgements from time to time as to whether particular behaviours constitute 'wrongdoing' and whether these have caused harm or are, at least potentially, harmful. When such judgements are made, staff will need to consider how best to intervene.

It can be argued that when one person is judged to have harmed another, the act of harming results in a moral inequality between the person responsible and the person harmed. The person who has caused harm to another has, as a result, weakened their own moral authority in relation to the other individual and perhaps in the broader community. A restorative process that aims to address this harm needs to take account of this moral imbalance, otherwise the person who has been harmed risks being further harmed by their experience of the process.

Example

Consider a situation in which one person has assaulted another. If the purpose of the intervention is to address the harm done, then there needs to be an acknowledgement within the process that the assault was 'morally wrong'. It would clearly not be appropriate to ask the person harmed to participate in any process that implies that they had an equal moral responsibility for the assault.

Where clear harm has been done, using an intervention that implies that the person who has been harmed is equally responsible for the harmful act would send confusing or contradictory messages about the school's and the community's value base. Of course, there may be an underlying conflict or provocation that led to the assault and it may well be that this aspect also needs to be addressed as part of, or subsequent to, the intervention. Therefore, any Restorative Intervention should allow for the possibility that as new information comes to light, we may need to change the intervention's purpose or process in order to meet the needs of all those affected.

Addressing harm, conflict and communication breakdown: which comes first?

If people are feeling harmed and/or are in conflict, then it is often the case that they are no longer able to communicate constructively with each other. Where such communication breakdown occurs, it becomes much less likely that those affected will spontaneously repair their relationship. A structured and managed intervention can help to re-establish constructive communication. And so a key role for anyone intervening is to identify what kind of process will best meet the needs of those individuals involved or affected. Chapter 6 will explore in detail the range of Restorative Interventions that are available and also the decision-making processes that will help determine what kind of intervention to offer.

Most schools communicate the values that they wish their learners to adopt through some kind of public declaration, often in the form of value statements, aims, 'golden rules' or 'codes of conduct'. For simplicity's sake we will consider all of these under the broad term 'rules'. How, then, does Restorative Practice address incidents of rule breaking? To consider this we first need to ask a broader question: *What are school rules for?*

What are your rules for?

The way in which we create, articulate and apply rules in schools teaches our children a great deal – not just about how we would like them to behave, but also about staff attitudes and beliefs, and about the wider societal values.

Why do schools have rules? In all likelihood a school's rules will fulfil a number of different purposes in relation to a range of contexts. Table 4.2 gives some typical examples of school rules, identifies their possible purposes and suggests a specific context for each.

Clearly, some rules will serve more than one purpose and will encompass more than one context. Many rules are designed to establish safe and appropriate behaviours. By definition, the breaking of any rule with this purpose implies at least the possibility that someone will feel harmed as a consequence of the rule-breaking behaviour.

In recent years, schools have been encouraged to create classroom and school rules in more participative ways by establishing consensus through consultation with pupils and parents, rather than simply imposing rules as predetermined givens. This approach encourages shared understanding and ownership of the rules, and may increase levels of compliance or adherence. This desired outcome may well be the motivation behind this democratization of the rule-making process in some schools. However, the establishing of any rule immediately raises the question *What will be the school's response to incidents of rule breaking?*

Table 4.2 School rules: purposes and contexts

Example rule	Purpose	Context
Bullying behaviour is not acceptable.	To ensure individual safety and appropriate relationships	The right to be free from harm
Walk on stairs and in corridors.	To ensure a safe learning environment	Health and safety
You should do as the teacher asks.	To ensure an educationally conducive climate	Quality of education
We should treat each other with respect.	To promote pro-social behaviour	Interpersonal relationships
You should wear school uniform.	To establish or reinforce a particular culture	Cultural values, beliefs or opinions

Traditionally, in UK schools the final resort, and sometimes the first resort, to rule breaking has been a retributive one.

A restorative perspective would assert that as long as the threat or use of sanctions remains the *principal* response to rule breaking, there will continue to be a cognitive gap between some students' *understanding* of the rules and their understanding of the *impact of their rule-breaking behaviour*. This is important because a child who not only understands the meaning of a rule but also understands its purpose, in terms of the impact of rule-breaking behaviour on others, is more likely to act pro-socially. This is in stark contrast to children who adhere to rules either for the rule's sake or for fear of sanctions. In other words, children are more likely to behave in ways that meet the expectations of the rule if they see that particular behaviour as socially appropriate and in keeping with their own moral code.

Reflection

Consider the act of stealing as an example of rule-breaking behaviour.

Do you steal? If not, why not?

Most people do not steal because they understand that stealing has a detrimental impact on the person (or organization) being stolen from. This is an example of pro-social behaviour.

Do we want children to refrain from stealing for the same pro-social reasons? Or do we want them to refrain from stealing simply because we tell them it is wrong, or because they are afraid of the associated sanction if they are caught?

How effective are your rules and sanctions?

It may be useful to consider how effective sanctions are at encouraging rule adherence in your school. The questionnaire set out in Table 4.3 is intended to allow you to explore these issues in more depth. It is based on an experiential training exercise that can provide a useful starting point in staff discussions about rules in relation to Restorative Practice.

Staff responses to this exercise often highlight what appears to be an inherent contradiction in sanctions-based responses to rule breaking. This can perhaps best be summarized as follows:

> We feel the *need to rely* on sanctions. At the very least, sanctions demonstrate the importance that we give to our rules. However, sanction systems seem inevitably to be marred by problems of inconsistency

Table 4.3 Rules questionnaire

Statement	Agree strongly	Agree	Disagree	Disagree strongly
I think schools need rules to operate effectively.				
Without sanctions, rules would be difficult to enforce.				
The majority of our students follow the most important rules most of the time.				
I think all of our current school rules are necessary, appropriate, fair and enforceable.				
Sanctions are a useful way to encourage students to follow the rules.				
The main reason that *some* students follow rules is that they are afraid to break them.				
Fear of rule breaking is a good way to manage students' behaviour.				
Sanctions are least effective for those students who break the rules most often.				
Our existing sanctions help all our students to take responsibility for their own behaviour and its impact on others.				

and ineffectiveness. They tend to induce fear in some students. We recognize these features of sanctions-based systems as undesirable and unhelpful to learning, but are 'stuck' with them, for lack of a more effective approach.

How did we come to rely on sanctions-based approaches that so clearly fail to meet both our aspirations for our schools and the needs of our students?

Rule breaking and wrongdoing in a retributive culture

In a retributive culture, 'wrongdoing' is defined principally by the breaking of rules. However derived, these rules will generally be represented as the collective views and expectations of the institution or school community. Therefore, rule breaking is often seen principally as an *offence against the institution* or against the community. Consequently, sanctions are administered by those in positions of power (staff) *on behalf of the institution*. In this conceptualization of wrongdoing, the rule serves as a 'line in the sand'. When you cross the line, a sanction is the inevitable 'consequence' – if you are caught! This teaches our children that a consequence is always negative and potentially avoidable.

There can be concern among staff and parents that any failure to administer sanctions in a consistent manner will indicate a weakness in the authority of the institution (the school) and therefore a weakness in the authority of those who represent it (the teachers). The net effect of this way of thinking is to leave teachers with an irresolvable dilemma:

- On the one hand, any inconsistent application of sanctions runs the risk of generating feelings of unfairness on the part of the recipient and bystanders. Children can learn that the breaking of a given rule may not always result in the associated sanction. Children who have done something wrong and who detect such inconsistencies may put their energies into avoiding getting caught, playing on adult sympathies or 'working the system'. As a result, the focus of the child's thinking is on avoiding the sanction rather than on understanding and taking responsibility for their behaviour.
- On the other hand, as caring, responsive and inclusive professionals we need to have regard for any mitigating circumstances (individual needs, prior histories, learned behaviours, and so on) of those involved in incidents of rule breaking when considering how best to respond. The desire to differentiate the response in the light of individual factors is an understandable and humane approach. Most teachers become very uncomfortable if they are not given leeway to use their professional judgement when addressing wrongdoing. The application of sanctions with absolute consistency, regardless of individual circumstances, leads at best to an inflexible response and at worst to a dehumanizing experience.

In reality, every headteacher knows that there are always issues around the inconsistent use of sanctions in schools. Instead of investing large amounts of our time and effort in resolving what is an inherent contradiction of sanctions-based systems, now is the time to rethink how we perceive rule breaking and wrongdoing.

Summary

In a retributive culture the 'consequence' of a misdemeanour is the sanction you receive as a result of being caught.

Rule breaking and wrongdoing in a restorative culture

In a restorative culture, wrongdoing is defined in terms of the harm or potential harm that one's behaviour causes others. When a rule is broken, the 'offence' is against the *individual* rather than against the *institution*.

What about incidents of rule breaking where there is no obvious direct harm to another person?

There are commonly three contexts where this may be the case – situations of:

- potential harm;
- indirect harm; or
- arguable harm.

The following illustrations of rule breaking will help to clarify these distinctions.

Illustration 1: Breaking a window – potential harm

The child who breaks a window may rationalize that no one was harmed by this event. However, it is not difficult to explore the potential for someone to have been harmed, and the possibility of harming someone in the future if the behaviour is repeated. In such a case, an appropriate member of staff could be involved in a Restorative Intervention to represent a person potentially harmed. (Also, harm has in fact been done because of the cost, work and inconvenience required to repair the window.)

Illustration 2: Graffiti in the toilets – indirect harm

Again, a child who has written obscene graffiti on the toilet wall may rationalize that no one in particular was harmed by this behaviour. However, there will be cost, work and inconvenience incurred in removing it. In such a case, an appropriate member of staff such as the janitor could be involved in a Restorative Intervention as the person harmed. (Also, some individuals might be deeply offended by what has been written.)

Illustration 3: Not wearing school uniform – arguable harm

In the case of not wearing school uniform, it might prove more difficult to explain who has been harmed by such behaviour. Where the context for a rule relates to cultural values, beliefs or opinions and where the case for harm is arguable, it is unlikely that a Restorative Intervention will prove productive. Mediation may be more appropriate.

In a restorative culture, rules are seen not as 'lines in the sand', but as 'guide rails' against which we can measure our own behaviour. Seeing rules in this way can help us to develop and maintain safe and respectful interactions. When our actions lead us to drift away from these guide rails, the consequence of our behaviour is not defined in terms of the rule that has been broken and the associated sanction, but instead described in terms of the consequence of that behaviour for others and for ourselves.

Summary

In a restorative culture, the consequence of a misdemeanour is the harmful impact of the behaviour on those affected.

The implementation of Restorative Practice requires us to think carefully not only about the rules that we have in schools, and how we respond to rule breaking, but also about the kinds of learning we want our children to experience in relation to rules. Ultimately, pro-social behaviour is the cornerstone of responsible citizenship. Restorative Practice provides a powerful framework for the development of pro-social understanding. In Chapter 5 we shall consider some of the proactive approaches that can help schools to build the foundations of this framework.

Where do sanctions fit in?

We know from research that a school's reliance on sanctions can be dramatically reduced as Restorative Practice is embedded in the life of the school. Indeed, some schools have effectively removed their use of sanctions, finding more restorative ways to respond to all incidents and concerns. This suggests an important question: *Can Restorative Approaches and sanctions run alongside each other harmoniously?*

The honest answer to this question is 'No'. The values, attitudes and beliefs of a genuinely restorative culture are at odds with one that condones the use of sanctions. Restorative Practice will be most effective in schools that commit themselves, over time, to its full implications.

In practical terms, however, we also know that it is unrealistic to expect schools to abandon sanctions-based approaches overnight and so there will inevitably be a transition period during which sanctions and Restorative Approaches need to coexist. It is important to recognize that child, parent and staff attitudes and understanding can take a significant time to shift. It is equally important to recognize that for some people it is through experiencing Restorative Approaches that attitudinal change and shared understanding develop fastest.

A note of caution...

A guiding principle where sanctions are still being used alongside Restorative Approaches is to be open and 'up front' about the sanctions. Where a child's behaviour is deemed to require a sanctions-based response, and where the school also wishes to offer a restorative response, staff should be open about this with the child from the outset. A child who suspects that a sanction is going to be imposed but has not been told so is unlikely to commit genuinely to a Restorative Intervention when it is offered. Telling a child that they will receive a sanction and then asking them to take part in a restorative process carries no guarantees of success, but it is more likely to be perceived as a genuine response than the reverse option.

Chapter 5

Proactive approaches

Before we can ask to draw on a child's reserve of resilience, we first need
to help them top up the tank.
(From an idea described by Marg Thorsborne)

This chapter covers:

Curriculum-based programmes (conflict resolution and emotional
literacy)
Circle-based approaches
Who can use circles?
Buddying and befriending
Mentoring
Proactive or responsive? Some grey areas explored
A common thread

We are all familiar with the idea that prevention is better than cure. However,
the proactive approaches considered in this chapter should be considered as
more than simply 'preventive measures' that schools might take to reduce the
incidence of conflict and harm among their learners. Proactive approaches can
play a central part in helping all children to develop as resilient individuals
with the capacities to build constructive relationships and to cope effectively
with conflict and harm. When the time comes to respond restoratively to specific incidents, responsive interventions place certain demands on the skills
and understanding of the young people involved. If we are not proactive in
helping children to develop their emotional articulacy and build up a personal
reserve of social and emotional resilience, how can we expect them to participate meaningfully in responsive interventions when these become necessary?

The existing range of proactive approaches that could be said to support
Restorative Practice is both wide and varied. This chapter aims to give an
overview of some of the principal approaches that are currently used in UK
schools, with some specific examples of practice. In selecting the examples

below, I do not mean to imply that other proactive approaches that have the same desired outcomes are not potentially of equal value.

Curriculum-based programmes

There are essentially two types of curriculum-based programmes that can support the whole-school development of Restorative Practice. These are:

1 conflict resolution skills programmes;
2 emotional intelligence programmes.

Conflict resolution skills programmes are generally designed as relatively short curriculum inserts delivered over a relatively small number of lessons (e.g. once a week for a school term) – usually as a part of the school's health and well-being curriculum, or its equivalent (e.g. personal, social and health education programmes). Such programmes focus on improving the abilities of all the children to manage conflict by:

- developing children's vocabulary in order to help them articulate their thoughts and feelings generally, and specifically when in conflict;
- building their conflict resolution skills (listening, empathy, turn taking, negotiating, being assertive, compromising);
- offering practical strategies (appropriate language and scripts, visualization, deep breathing).

Typically the focus is on helping children to:

- anticipate conflict, and recognize it when it occurs;
- understand that the way in which they respond can help to determine whether the conflict is escalated or de-escalated;
- learn to use conflict resolution skills.

An important part of any such programme is that the children learn experientially. This means there will be plenty of opportunities to role-play meaningful scenarios, share real experiences and try out different ways of thinking and responding.

A variety of conflict resolution programmes are available commercially. Some sources are given in the 'Resources' section of this book.

Emotional intelligence (also known as *emotional literacy* or *emotional resilience*) programmes take a broader and more holistic approach to child development, while incorporating much of what would be included in a typical conflict resolution programme. The aim here is to consciously embed the development of the child's emotional intelligence within the curriculum content and experiences throughout their time in school. As such, these programmes are not seen solely as part of the health and well-being programme, but rather as an essential, cross-curricular approach that links the practicalities of day-to-day relationships in school with the more high-minded aspirations towards responsible citizenship. In this holistic approach, emotional intelligence can be seen as underpinning effective learning and teaching.

An example of such a programme follows, to help illustrate the all-encompassing reach of this proactive approach. Further information about this programme can be found in the 'Resources' section.

Example of a curricular programme

'Being Cool in School' and 'What's Going On?' are the primary and secondary school components of a coherent, curricular programme for children aged from 4 to 14. Fife Council Education Service has devised the programme, and its implementation has complemented the introduction of a wide range of Restorative Approaches in its primary and secondary schools. The stated aim of the programme is to 'empower children to cope with the situations they encounter in their daily lives in school and beyond'.

Through a planned programme of activities, including discussion, reflection, healthy introspection and role play, a range of skills and concepts are introduced, reinforced and progressively developed. Children learn the difference between passive, aggressive and assertive ways of relating to others and practise helpful, assertive ways of responding to conflict.

The primary school programme has been mapped to national educational priorities and curriculum guidelines covering relevant aspects of emotional health, physical and social health, English language, expressive arts, and religious and moral education. Completion of the secondary school version can contribute towards national qualifications in a number of curricular areas.

Evaluations with Fife and other Scottish education services have demonstrated that children engaged in the programme become more able to resolve difficult situations and conflicts themselves. There have been measurable reductions in:

- incidences of challenging behaviour in class;
- referrals from the playground;
- demands on staff time to deal with incidents.

Circle-based approaches

The roots of current Restorative Practice lie in the community circles that have been used for centuries by indigenous peoples in some countries, such as community healing circles in Maori culture. There is clearly common ground between the core principles outlined above and those of a Restorative Approach. Circle-based approaches can form an integral part of curriculum-based programmes.

The considerable potential of circle-based approaches to help us learn about ourselves and about our relationships has been recognized outside schools for many years. Circles have been used in a wide variety of contexts for adults and children including in psychotherapy, counselling and other mental health fields, in social work practice and in groups addressing addictive, self-harming and abusive behaviours.

Most circle work is based on a few clear principles. Typically:

- Participation in the circle is voluntary.
- Everyone in the circle has the right to contribute equally to the work of the circle, and any contributions should be valued equally.
- There should be no requirement or pressure placed on individuals to speak. Each takes responsibility for their contribution.
- Individuals should show respect for others in the circle.

Beyond these four basic tenets, the participants decide what ground rules and practical arrangements will apply to the work of the circle.

Probably the most comprehensive and best-known approach to circle work in UK schools is 'Quality Circle Time'. This is a whole-school approach based on the use of circles that has been devised and promoted since the mid-1990s by Jenny Mosley Consultancies (See the 'Resources' section for more information). While Quality Circle Time shares many of the values, aspirations and skills of Restorative Practice, the use of sanctions (e.g. partial withdrawal of 'golden time') as a way of responding to undesirable behaviours sets it aside from a fully Restorative Approach.

Most circles use a 'talking object' to encourage appropriate participation. This is a symbolic object (it could be a ball, a beanbag, a soft toy, etc.), possession of which allows the holder, and no one else, to speak to the circle. Depending on the type of circle activity, the talking object may be passed consecutively around the circle or, on request, passed from person to person across the circle.

In schools there are broadly two types of circles, distinguished by their purposes, which could be described as taking a proactive approach: community building circles and checking-in circles.

Community building circles are circles in which the facilitator offers specific activities that will help the participants to develop a range of pro-social qualities and skills, including:

- confidence in participating in a group;
- turn taking;
- communication skills, including assertiveness;
- empathy;
- mutual support;
- a sense of belonging.

The activities offered are often in the form of games that help to increase enjoyment and participation in a non-threatening way.

Checking-in circles create an opportunity for all those in the circle to 'check in' before other activities are undertaken. Typically, a class teacher will use a checking-in circle at the start of each school day. The purpose of this circle activity is to give the members of a group or class time to bring up any concerns, queries or relevant information that will help the others in the circle, including any school staff, to be supportive of each other.

This activity may be initiated by participants being asked to respond, if they wish, to an opening question such as 'How are you feeling about school today?' Alternatively, the class may be comfortable enough with the format and process to spontaneously raise any issues, if they wish. 'Checking-out' circles are also used in some schools to mark the end of the day.

Two further types of circle that are being used in schools are:

- problem-solving circles (to be considered later in this chapter under the heading 'Proactive or responsive? Some grey areas');
- restorative circles (considered in Chapter 6).

Who can use circles?

All school staff can learn to use circles. Children of nursery age upwards can learn to participate in circles. However, there can be some practical and emotional barriers to be overcome if circle work is to be genuinely embraced by the staff of a school.

While the format of circle work may at first glance seem to lend itself more to a primary school setting, there is no significant reason why the approach cannot be used in secondary schools to equal effect. The culture of circle work can appear alien to those who work in secondary schools (with some notable examples, such as drama and physical education teachers), and there are certain concerns that are commonly raised when introducing the approach. Table 5.1 lists some of these and offers some responses that can help to address these anxieties.

Table 5.1 Concerns about using circles

Concern	Response
We don't have time in secondary schools to interrupt the curriculum in order to do circles.	Opportunities may already exist for circles to take place (e.g. registration or form periods). The potential benefits of circle work can outweigh the time costs.
The layout and furniture in secondary school classrooms do not lend themselves to circle work.	Modern classrooms generally have furnishings that can be arranged flexibly. As with any routine, children can learn to set up and dismantle a circle quite speedily. The act of creating a circle is a cooperative exercise in itself. While it may take a minute or two to organize a circle, the longer-term results may well be worth the time and disruption involved. Where a 'proper' circle (i.e. chairs only) is impracticable, an informal circle (e.g. children standing around the edges of the room) may suffice.
Working in circles can be an uncomfortable experience for secondary school teachers.	As with all Restorative Approaches, staff should be appropriately trained and supported when introducing new practice. The children may already be very comfortable with the idea of circles if they have experienced them at primary school.

Buddying and befriending

Buddying (sometimes known as befriending) is a form of peer support that has been increasingly adopted by both primary and secondary schools in recent years. Buddy schemes often involve older children in buddying younger ones with the aim of creating positive relationships and giving reassurance or support to identified groups of children. There are many different contexts for buddying but all share some common themes:

- Buddying provides children with peers who can provide practical, social and emotional support.
- Buddies can provide positive role models that can help younger or vulnerable children to learn more pro-social ways of relating to their peers.
- Buddying helps to break down the artificial age-based social stratification that is an inevitable consequence of schools organizing children into age-related learning groups.

Children who are to take on the role of buddies need appropriate preparation, training and ongoing support to ensure that they:

- can use appropriate interpersonal skills;
- understand the purpose and boundaries of their role;

- are not put in difficult or inappropriate positions;
- know when to refer concerns on to an adult.

Schools need to prepare carefully for introducing buddies if they are to be effective and safe. The guide sheet that follows is designed to support schools in planning a buddy scheme.

Planning a buddy programme

Consultation

Key questions for this stage are:

- Why is buddying being considered in your school?
- What kind of buddying do you plan to introduce?
- Specifically, what kinds of benefits will the scheme offer its users?
- Who will be considered as potential buddies and how will they be selected?
- Who will be considered as users and how will they be selected?
- In what ways will the different parts of the school community be involved in planning a scheme?
- How will members of the school community be informed of the scheme?

The following people will need to be involved:

- *All children*: All children need to understand the purpose of introducing buddying – who will be involved, what it is for and what it is not for.
- *Buddies*: Buddies need to understand what is expected of them, what are the boundaries to their work and how they will be supported.
- *Users*: Those who are being 'buddied' need to know what is on offer and how they can make best use of the service.
- *Staff*: Staff should be aware of the above issues in order to support the scheme effectively and to allay any concerns regarding either overlap with other support mechanisms or the demands being placed on the buddies.
- *Parents*: Parents, particularly of the buddies, may have concerns about what is being asked or expected of their children. They may wonder why their children have been chosen as buddies or to be buddied.

Once these issues have been addressed, the following stages will need to be planned:

Preparation

Preparation will include the selection of buddies, the planning of training, practical arrangements and agreeing ongoing support.

Training and launch

Who will deliver training – in-house or external staff?
    As part of their training, buddies will typically:

- clarify their role as buddies;
- understand how the scheme will operate;
- practise experientially the basic buddying skills of active listening and empathy, and develop relevant support strategies;
- know when and how to involve an adult;
- understand how they will be supported in their work by staff.

There are a number of types of buddying schemes. Brief examples of the most common types are described below.

Cross-class buddies: Every week a group of older buddies works one to one with their allocated younger buddies on a particular task or activity – planned and supported by the class teachers of both groups. This might include paired reading, playing maths games, craftwork, musical activities, and so on.

Playground buddies: Trained buddies are 'on call' on a rota basis during break times. They can be identified by other children by their caps, sashes, badges, etc. and/or can be found at a particular location (e.g. at a 'friendship stop' in the playground, or in an accessible, 'drop in' room in the school building). Other children who have a concern or a worry, or need help, can approach them for support. In primary schools the buddies may have a role in encouraging younger children to play and to use games equipment appropriately.

Transition buddies: Older children are allocated to small groups of new arrivals at the start of the school year. The buddies' role is to escort the new children around the school at changeovers for the first few days to help them orientate themselves. They may also meet up regularly (e.g. once a week in registration/form time) to find out how they are settling in and to check whether they have any concerns or questions about the school.

Mentoring

Mentoring has been defined in many ways. A useful definition, for the purposes of this book is as follows:

> In practice, mentors provide a spectrum of learning and supporting behaviours, from challenging and being a critical friend to being a role model, from helping to build networks and develop personal resourcefulness to simply being there to listen, from helping people work out what they want to achieve, and why, to planning how they will bring change about.
> (David Clutterbuck, Scottish Mentoring Network, 2008)

Mentoring is established practice in many fields of adult life. It includes workplace mentoring, and mentoring to support employability skills. In schools the role of mentor to a child can be fulfilled by at least three different groups of individuals: fellow children (peers), staff, and other adults not employed to work in the school. Mentors often work one to one with their mentees, but mentoring groups also exist in some schools. Most school mentoring schemes are offered for a fixed time period (e.g. for one term), rather than for an indeterminate period.

As with buddying, there are some common themes to all mentoring activity, regardless of who fulfils the role:

- Mentoring is a voluntary activity for mentor and mentee.
- Mentors provide a range of supports, from a listening ear through to practical advice and support with goal setting.
- Part of the mentor's role is to be a positive role model.

Mentoring can be offered to all those in a particular group (e.g. a year group) or may be targeted for certain individuals, based on given criteria. Brief examples of some typical schemes are given below.

Peer mentoring

In a secondary school, students who are struggling to form effective peer-group relationships are given the opportunity to be attached to small mentoring groups (up to four children) which are mentored by two child mentors. They meet as a group regularly to undertake activities (games, homework support), to talk about their progress and to get advice and ideas about how to relate effectively. The dynamics of the group are designed to model and develop effective communication and relational skills.

Staff mentoring

Children who are regularly getting into difficulties with their behaviour or attainment are offered a one-to-one mentor drawn from volunteer staff. This may be a member of staff who already has a positive relationship with the child, or it may be someone new to the child. The mentor meets with the child at least weekly to explore concerns, to help the mentee establish relevant goals and/or targets and to review and amend these targets as appropriate.

Other adult mentoring

Children in a secondary school who are approaching school leaving age and are struggling to identify clear 'next steps' have an opportunity to meet with a mentor from 'the world of work'. This is an adult volunteer who meets with mentees in order to explore with the mentee aspects of life beyond school, including anxieties about 'moving on', the challenges of the workplace and career development, the skills and attributes that will be required, etc. The mentor serves as a positive role model, helping to build the confidence of the mentee.

As with buddying, mentors will need appropriate training, and schools will need to take care in planning, implementing and supporting any mentoring scheme. The guidance given earlier for planning a buddying programme can be easily adapted for mentoring schemes.

Proactive or responsive? Some grey areas explored

When does a proactive approach stop being proactive?

A 'whole-school' approach means a WHOLE-SCHOOL approach. The evidence from research to date suggests that if we limit access to these approaches to certain groups of children, we deny the potential benefits to all, and risk undermining the values and philosophy that underpin Restorative Practice.

Nonetheless, there are examples where proactive approaches have been successfully adapted and offered to those with particular needs, albeit alongside whole-school programmes. Some examples of this way of working are outlined in Table 5.2.

Table 5.2 Responsive adaptations to proactive approaches

Proactive approach	*Responsive adaptation*
Conflict resolution programmes	Where particular children are having difficulty avoiding or handling conflict, programmes can be tailored or delivered in a more focused way to address issues such as: • expressing one's own emotions; • reading others' emotional signals; • reacting appropriately to stressful situations; • aspects of anger management. Tailored programmes may be of benefit to children who experience a lot of conflict out of school or who have difficulty in understanding the emotions of others (e.g. as in Asperger's syndrome).
Circle-based approaches	Circle processes can be a very effective way of helping groups to problem-solve collectively. Children who are already used to using circles to build a sense of community and for checking in will find it relatively easy to work collaboratively to solve problems and meet challenges set for the group. Simple problem-solving models can be adapted successfully to fit within the circle process.
Buddying	Buddying can be used successfully to support identified individuals in circumstances such as: • new arrivals during the school year; • children arriving in the school who have previously had difficult peer relationships; • children currently in the school who have become vulnerable to peer pressure or who are having difficulty relating positively to their peers. In all these cases, and probably in any other similar ones that might be conceived, it is *essential* that the young buddy is not given an inappropriate role or responsibility. The buddying support that is provided should only be a small part of the support package offered by the school community to the child in need. The existence of buddy support in a school should be an asset, but not a replacement for adult support.
Mentoring	Mentoring often has a targeted component aiming to support particular groups of children or individuals. Thus, it is as likely in some ways to have responsive elements to its function, as it is to be proactive.

A common thread

This chapter has introduced a range of proactive approaches that can complement and support the implementation of Restorative Practice in a school. The range reviewed here is not exhaustive. There is no prescriptive suite of proactive approaches guaranteed to create the kind of climate in which Restorative Practice will thrive. Schools need to devise creative ways of working proactively with children to develop their emotional intelligence in order to suit the needs of different children, schools and cultures.

It is possible, nonetheless, to identify a common thread that runs through those approaches that are most supportive of Restorative Practice. Clearly, these approaches will need to develop and echo the values and attitudes that are inherent in restorative thinking (see Chapter 3). However, the thread that runs common to both the Proactive and the responsive 'branches' of Restorative Practice is, perhaps, their person-centredness.

This book is not the place to explore person-centred theory in depth, but I believe that there is good evidence that both branches of Restorative Practice (proactive and responsive) succeed because they offer those involved the 'core conditions' of a person-centred relationship. Carl Rogers first defined these core conditions in his influential work on person-centred theory in the 1950s and 1960s. Much of this theory has, over time, become subsumed (and sometimes distorted) into educational practice, as well as into the work of various other helping professions.

Rogers argued that in order to develop a healthy self-concept, we need to experience three core conditions in our relationships with those around us. An understanding of what the core conditions of a helping relationship are, and why they matter, will help you to identify other proactive approaches that are likely to support the development of Restorative Practice. For this reason, a brief summary of these ideas is given in the next box. More information on person-centred theory can be found via the 'Resources' section of this book.

Why do these core conditions matter?

How can children learn to understand how someone else feels – to be empathic – if they do not experience empathy from others? How can children learn to value themselves and others as unique individuals if we cannot value them for who they truly are? How can we ask children to be honest and open with us if we are not offering them an honest reflection of who we are, what we think and how we feel?

The core conditions

Empathy

Empathy involves one person striving to understand how another actually experiences some part of his or her life. Rogers argued that we can never know exactly how someone else feels because of the unique nature of individual experience, but at its most powerful, empathy involves experiencing 'as if' the experience were your own. The attempt to understand empathically has a powerful effect on the self-concept of both giver and receiver.

Rogers made a clear distinction between *empathy* and *sympathy*. When you sympathize with someone, you generally work from *your own* perspective – e.g. 'I feel sorry for you.' You may identify with the other's position – 'I've been there too.' You may feel inclined to take sides – 'I'm not surprised you feel like that. That's exactly how I would feel!'

Being empathic requires us instead to temporarily lay aside those aspects of our own experience that may distort what we are trying to perceive in the other person. But to be helpful it is not enough to *feel* empathic with someone. We must also find ways of communicating our empathy. When we experience empathy from others, we feel that we are understood; that we are not alone; that our feelings have some legitimacy; and that someone is prepared to be with us when things are difficult.

Unconditional positive regard

Although the terminology may be unfamiliar, the concepts encompassed by 'unconditional positive regard' will be familiar to most people. It involves the ability to communicate your regard for a person without the imposition by you of any conditions on that regard. You can accept someone the way they are. You may not approve of their attitudes, agree with their values or condone their behaviour but the person matters to you nonetheless. Related terms that are often used when describing positive regard include acceptance, warmth, respect and valuing.

When we are offered unconditional positive regard, we feel that we matter; that someone else is there for us; that we have permission to be honest about our feelings; that the parts of us that we feel are unacceptable can be experienced; that we are potentially acceptable as fellow beings.

Congruence

Rogers saw congruence in some respects as the most challenging of the core conditions. The congruence he describes is an *internal* one (intrapersonal), not that between people (interpersonal), and so should not be confused with empathy. You are congruent when that which you are experiencing at the time on the inside is honestly and openly communicated on the outside. Your outward signals, verbal language and body language accurately represent what you are feeling and thinking. There is a lack of covering up, deception, collusion, manipulation or hidden agendas. Related terms that are often used when describing congruence include honesty, genuineness, transparency and realness.

When we are with someone who is being congruent, we feel we can trust them; that they can be relied on to be honest with us, that it might be ok for us to be honest with ourselves and with others.

In this chapter we have reviewed the range of proactive approaches that will support Restorative Practice in schools. Chapter 6 explores the restorative responses that schools can make when things go wrong between people.

Responsive approaches: when things go wrong between people

This chapter considers:

Mediation and Restorative Justice-based interventions
Repairing relationships
Why intervene? What are the needs?
Mediation: the basics
Mediation in schools: process and examples
Restorative Interventions: the basics
The impact of harmful behaviour: encouraging personal responsibility
Restorative Interventions: conversations, meetings, circles and conferences
Restorative enquiry
Who, when and where?
Other supportive interventions
Deciding which response is appropriate

Mediation and Restorative Justice-based interventions

In considering Restorative Practice, this book recognizes that responsive approaches, in the United Kingdom at least, have evolved out of two main processes: Mediation and Restorative Justice-based Interventions (hereafter Restorative Interventions). Each of these processes has its own developmental background (see Chapter 2) and is used in different contexts outside schools. Variations on each process are also currently practised within schools in a variety of contexts.

Mediation and Restorative Interventions differ primarily in their *purposes* and in the consequent *frameworks* that are used to manage the processes. (A summary of the key differences will be given at the end of this chapter.) There is ongoing debate within the Restorative Practice community as to whether Mediation and Restorative Intervention processes can and should be merged or blended to provide a single intervention framework for schools (for example, see 'Restorative Enquiry', p. 100). Such a unified approach has some appeal, not least because of its simplicity.

However, since distinctive examples of both processes are already being used in schools in the United Kingdom, we will consider each process separately. We will also consider the practical implications for schools in adopting the two types of intervention and why maintaining a distinction in the purpose of any intervention is important.

Despite the distinctions, Mediation and Restorative Interventions have a number of common features:

- They are voluntary processes.
- All those affected can actively participate in the process.
- They are each based on clear, although to some degree distinctive, theoretical frameworks that have developed out of practice.
- Trained, impartial facilitators, who can be school staff, generally manage the processes.
- Many of the skills that the facilitator needs are common to both processes.

Before we look at these processes in detail, it is worth considering an important question that lies at the heart of all restorative processes.

Repairing relationships

Where a relationship between other people has been damaged or has broken down, what can be done to repair it?

If people are feeling harmed or are in conflict, spontaneous repairing of the relationship is often no longer feasible because they are no longer able to communicate constructively with each other. A more structured and managed framework for communication is needed. The role of the person intervening is to identify a process that will help participants to communicate and will allow them to address the harm or conflict effectively. A facilitator can help to create a climate within which those involved may choose to build bridges in their damaged relationship. This climate can be nurtured through the use of appropriate skills and processes.

A facilitator intervening in an interpersonal process does not have the power or gift to 'repair' a relationship. Ultimately, the repairing of any relationship is entirely and wholly in the control of those involved in that relationship. If a facilitator agrees to take responsibility for 'repairing a relationship', this implies a process that would be contrary to one of the principles of Restorative Practice, which requires that a process is 'done with' the participants rather than 'done to' them.

As we explored in Chapter 4, when things go wrong between people it is not always easy to disentangle feelings of harm, sources of conflict and problems of communication. However, we need to have regard to these distinctions if an appropriate and helpful intervention is to be offered. In order to establish a restorative climate, a member of staff intervening in any interpersonal problem needs to consider two key questions:

1   What presenting need(s) do the participants want to address?

Then:

2   What skills and processes can I offer in order to best address these needs?

Why intervene? What are the needs?

Anyone intervening in an interpersonal problem in schools needs to have regard for the individual needs of participants – first and foremost their needs for safety, respect, support and appropriate confidentiality. Any responsive approach designed to address conflict or harm should take all of these basic needs into account. However, in any context requiring an intervention, there are likely to be other needs arising from the previous interactions of those who have been affected. The responsive approaches that we consider in this chapter are designed variously to address the following presenting needs of the participants:

1   their need to address any perceived HARM done;
2   their need to resolve any ongoing CONFLICT;
3   their need to establish more constructive COMMUNICATION.

If more than one of these needs is significant, then the person intervening will need to work with those involved to prioritize their needs and to decide which can be addressed through any given intervention. This process of prioritization will help determine which type of intervention is appropriate. While this may seem a rather mechanistic way of approaching the problem, I would suggest that this 'filtering' process is one that all effective restorative practitioners undertake, whether overtly and consciously or otherwise. Why is this filtering important?

Example

Imagine a situation where constructive communication has broken down between two children because of an ongoing conflict, for example a falling out that leads to a refusal to participate in some activity. It may well be that the conflict needs to be addressed first if effective communication and participation are to be re-established. Mediation could help to resolve this conflict.

Similarly, imagine a situation where an escalating conflict between two people has led one to harm the other (or both to harm each other): for example, where one student has assaulted another following a dispute over ownership of property. It may prove difficult to resolve the underlying conflict unless their individual needs arising from the 'harm done' are addressed first. A Restorative face-to-face Meeting could address these needs.

Unpacking the spiral

Communication breakdown, conflict and harm can form a self-perpetuating and damaging spiral, and so interpersonal problems can escalate and become more entrenched. If people are to repair their damaged relationships, then they may need help unpacking the spiral (see Figure 6.1).

If we start by identifying the participants' presenting needs, then we reduce the risk of an intervention making matters worse. A skilled facilitator will help the participants to identify what needs to be addressed first, and then what process will best allow them to address these needs. It would be inappropriate, and potentially harmful, if we brought together people whose presenting needs were incompatible.

Example

Where one person's presenting need is to make an apology and reparation for the harm they have done, while the other's presenting need is for retribution, then a Restorative Intervention is likely to increase feelings of frustration and harm, rather than to address these.

Human relationships can be very complex, and it is possible in some cases that all three needs may coexist (their need to address any perceived HARM

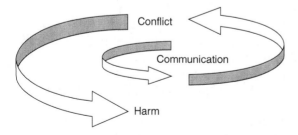

Figure 6.1 Communication breakdown, conflict and harm: unpacking the spiral

done, their need to resolve any ongoing CONFLICT and their need to establish more constructive COMMUNICATION). In such a context, the need to address these appropriately can be illustrated with the help of an analogy.

An analogy

Imagine I have developed a habit of regularly bumping my car on the kerb when I steer it into the driveway of my house. My inappropriate driving behaviour has resulted in my front tyres becoming misaligned. Over time, this misalignment (conflict) has led to uneven wear on the treads of these tyres (harm), to the point where driving on wet roads has become dangerous.

If I take the car to a mechanic to have the problem attended to, then there are three ways in which I can be helped:

1   The damaged tyres can be replaced – addressing the harm done.
2   The wheel alignment can be corrected – resolving the conflict between the tyres.
3   I can be helped to understand how I am responsible for causing the damage, in the hope that I will change my approach to the driveway. This will involve me in changing my behaviour – 'communicating' more effectively with my car.

In this analogy I can tackle the issue in three different ways, but all three forms of help will be necessary if the car is to be made safe and if I am going to learn how to avoid the problem in the future. Replacing the tyres (addressing the harm done) is perhaps the most urgent purpose of any intervention. However, if the tyre alignment is not corrected, then this conflict will continue to cause harm. And finally, without a change in my driving (communication skills and behaviour) I will continue to cause problems for myself in the future. I may be able to change my behaviour as a result of understanding how I have caused the problem. On the other hand, I may need to be shown how to enter my driveway correctly (i.e. I need to be taught the skill) in order for me to change my behaviour.

All analogies have their weak points. What this analogy clearly fails to convey is the dynamic complexity in the relationships between people (rather than between driver and car!) One of the strengths of any responsive approach is that, regardless of its primary purpose – addressing harm or resolving conflict – the process will also offer an opportunity for participants to:

• better understand each other;
• reflect on their own behaviour and its impact on others;
• improve the level and quality of their communication.

Bringing people together in a responsive approach is often the first step in re-establishing constructive communication, despite the fact that this is not necessarily the main focus of the restorative process itself. This is because we necessarily help to create a conducive climate for constructive communication when we offer an intervention that aims to resolve a conflict or address feelings of harm. The intervention may also help those involved to become more aware of any skill deficits that are contributing to the problematic behaviour. This awareness may in turn lead to other types of helpful intervention.

The analogy perhaps also fails to convey the degree to which the solutions to problems of harm, conflict and communication lie in the hands of the participants in a restorative process. Mechanics do things *to* cars. When we offer a responsive approach we can only do things *along with* the participants. When we replace a tyre, we can be reasonably confident that it will perform as required. Nothing is quite so certain when we offer to intervene in human relationships.

Of course, if we are to offer effective interventions, we need to have suitable skills. We also need to be able to offer suitable processes to match the participants' needs, and to be able to manage these processes effectively. (How to decide which type of intervention to offer is explored in more depth later in this chapter.) While appropriate skills and processes are necessary, they are not entirely sufficient. We also need to have some faith in each individual's capacity to make amends, to resolve conflicts or to change behaviours in the light of the better understanding that, hopefully, will result from the intervention. We may be tempted to use these skills and processes to try to engineer the outcomes that we wish for others, rather than to help them identify and achieve the outcomes that they wish for themselves. Some school staff find this shift to a facilitative role (one that aims to empower others rather than allow us to exert authority) quite challenging. For some it may represent an entirely new way of working with children. This emphasis on facilitative working will be explored in more detail in Chapter 7.

Mediation: the basics

Mediation is a way of resolving disputes by helping those involved to come to an agreement. It is often described as a conflict resolution process. It is characterized by a series of requirements and understandings:

1   Both parties need to agree to take part in order for mediation to take place. No aspect of the outcome is predetermined.
2   The participants decide the terms of any agreement, not the mediator.
3   The mediator is impartial and is, within ethical boundaries, 'morally neutral'; that is, a mediator does not speak or act as if either person is 'in the right' or 'in the wrong', except where ground rules for the mediation are being broken. See Chapter 4 for a more detailed discussion of this issue.

Summary

Mediation allows the participants to:

- take greater control of the existing conflict and any future resolution;
- communicate constructively about the conflict;
- generate an agreement that will help resolve the conflict.

The primary focus for the mediation process is on reaching an agreement about future actions or behaviours and/or improving mutual understanding.

Relationships may be repaired or reconciled, but this is not essential for a successful outcome for the participants. Participants can agree to disagree on some issues.

Apologies may be made by one or more participants, but this is not necessarily the case.

This mediation process has a proven track record in a number of contexts outside schools. Professional mediation services are used on a daily basis in many countries, including the United Kingdom, to help people to resolve disputes within families, neighbourhoods, in court proceedings and in workplace and international conflicts. Successful outcomes are reported, typically, in 70–85 per cent of face-to-face mediations, where the criterion for success is defined as the participants' satisfaction with the agreement at the time and in the longer term.

Mediation also has many potential applications in a school context. However, its purpose always remains the same: to help the participants resolve a dispute or conflict. For example, at the low-tariff end of the scale, Mediation may be offered to two children who are unable to resolve a minor fallout or disagreement in the playground. In this context, children themselves may be trained as the mediators (peer mediation). At the high-tariff end of the conflict scale, professional mediators may be brought in, for instance to help resolve an entrenched dispute between parents and an education service about provision for a child who needs significant additional support in school. In both these contexts the applied principles of mediation will be the same. However, the skill levels required of the facilitators and the time required for the processes will be very different.

Table 6.1 Summary of the Mediation process

Stage	Purpose
Referral	Those involved in the conflict get access to the Mediation service. This may be via self-referral or through recommendation by a third party.
Meeting person A	The mediator meets with person A to:
	• explain the mediation process and its purpose;
	• hear A's perception of the conflict;
	• explore the appropriateness of offering Mediation;
	• ensure that any participation is voluntary;
	• Help person A prepare for the Mediation meeting.
Meeting person B	The mediator meets with person B and covers the same issues as were covered with person A.
Bringing A and B together for a Mediation meeting	The mediator will:
	• explain the purpose and structure of the meeting;
	• ensure that both participants have come in good faith and are willing to work for an agreement;
	• ensure that key ground rules for the meeting are understood and accepted;
	• allow each person uninterrupted time in order for them to explain their perspective on the conflict;
	• work with the participants to identify interests, needs and any common ground;
	• encourage and support the participants in working toward a mutually acceptable agreement;
	• offer to record any agreement that has been reached.

Mediation in schools: process and examples

In practice, most mediation in schools follows a well-established process that has developed out of theory and practice. Table 6.1 summarizes the typical stages, and their purposes, of a mediation process. For simplicity, the process considered here is a conflict between two people: person A and person B.

In many mediation contexts, two mediators, working as co-facilitators, manage the process. There are several reasons for this arrangement. Some of these will be considered when we explore the idea of peer mediation.

In entrenched and difficult conflicts the success of any mediation often depends on the quality of the preparation that has been done with the participants in advance of their meeting together. In complex or high-tariff cases the preparation meetings with A and B may take place over more than one session. Bringing poorly prepared participants together may simply exacerbate the conflict rather than help resolve it.

Mediation between more than two participants in a conflict is possible, including between groups, but generally needs more careful preparation and places greater demands on the skills of the mediators in managing the process as a result of the more complex dynamics within a group.

Where the participants express a desire to work for an agreement but do not wish to meet face to face, an alternative process – shuttle mediation – may be offered. In this, the mediators act, with permission, as the 'carriers' of information and any proposed terms of agreement that have been given to them by each participant to be conveyed to the other. Clearly, this can be a more time-consuming process than face-to-face mediation and tends to have a lower success rate. In practice, shuttle mediation is rare in schools as the participants generally recognize the need to meet in order to establish future working relationships.

There are certain features of mediation that school staff who are new to the process can find surprising, and even challenging. These include the following:

- Mediators generally will not gather any background information from third parties about the prospective participants or their conflict, other than that required to ensure everyone's safety.
- Mediators, within ethical guidelines, offer confidentiality to the participants. It is entirely within the participants' control what information, if any, is shared with others about the mediation and any resulting agreement.
- It is fundamental to the mediation process that mediators do not provide or impose any solutions. School staff who are used to taking a more directive, problem-solving approach, or to 'fixing' problems for others, can find this aspect particularly challenging.

There are good reasons why these particular features are required in the mediation process, and each increases the likelihood of a successful outcome for the participants.

There are three further aspects, particularly relevant in school settings, that mediators need to pay attention to.

The first of these is the notion that mediators need to be impartial. This is a matter as much of perception and of intention. If a member of staff (or child, for that matter) offers to mediate in a conflict between two parties, and one or more of those parties believes that the mediator will favour the other party, then a genuine agreement is less likely to result. People who bring a conflict to the table, and talk openly about it in front of the other person involved, need to have confidence that the mediator(s) will not take sides and will provide appropriate support to all involved. Clearly, this can be a significant issue in some school contexts. For instance, a school's headteacher may have excellent mediation skills but is unlikely to be able to successfully mediate in a conflict between a class teacher and a parent if the parent perceives the primary role of the headteacher to be one of supporting the member of staff's position (see the example in the next box).

The second issue that needs careful consideration when mediating in school contexts is how best to address any imbalance of power between the participants. Schools, by their nature, involve power hierarchies. Typically there is a perceived chain of increasing power that starts perhaps at one end with children, then parents, then various 'layers' of school staff, then school managers, then education service managers. Even where a school strives to address these power imbalances during mediation, they remain an unavoidable reality in terms of professional responsibilities. Parents may also bring with them their personal history of power imbalances from their childhood experiences of school. It is a legitimate role for the mediator to consider and, where appropriate, to address such power imbalances, whether perceived or actual. The consideration of any power imbalances can be addressed in preparatory work with the participants by helping them to consider how each feels about the other person and how they might react in a meeting with them. The mediator also has a responsibility during the mediation meeting to ensure that power imbalances do not lead to unfair process, for instance where one participant attempts to dominate the dialogue or tries to impose a solution on the other.

Practical considerations, such as where and when a mediation process should take place, the layout of the room and so on, also have a part to play in setting a conducive climate for mediation.

The following example illustrates how, in failing to address issues of power imbalance and impartiality, an attempt at mediation could go badly wrong.

A failed attempt to mediate

A parent has contacted the headteacher of a school to complain that a class teacher has been 'picking on' their child in lessons. The headteacher promises to look into the concern and get back to the parent.

The headteacher discusses the complaint with the class teacher, whose perspective is that the child has not been working to the best of their ability and needs constant reminders and prompts to do the class work and homework. The headteacher sees this as an opportunity to use his mediation skills and suggests to the parent and the teacher that they 'get together for a chat to sort the problem out'. Both agree to this, and a time is fixed for an after-school meeting.

Both the parent and the teacher subsequently arrive at the meeting feeling somewhat apprehensive.

Problem: There has been no real preparation done with the individuals in advance of the meeting. The headteacher has not been clear with the participants about:

- the purpose of the meeting (exploratory, explanatory, looking for an agreement or apology?);
- the approach to be used (mediation, arbitration?);
- the role of the headteacher in this meeting (staff manager/supporter, representative of the education service, problem-solver, mediator?).

The headteacher invites the member of staff to sit with him at his table and the parent to sit opposite them both, on the other side of the table. The headteacher's chair is higher than either of the participants'.

Problem: The seating arrangements may convey to the parent that the staff are on one side of the argument while the parent is on the other. This may feel like 'two against one'. The position of the headteacher's chair may convey a sense of superiority.

During the meeting the headteacher gives both parties an opportunity to voice their concerns and then gives his perspective on the problem and suggests a solution. The parent gets angry and rejects his proposal, walking out of the meeting and saying, 'You teachers are all the same – you always back each other up and refuse to listen to what's really going on.'

Problem: The headteacher has started out in the role of a mediator without making this explicit to either participant, and then has switched to being an arbitrator. The parent experiences this lack of role clarity as confusing and unfair, and rejects the process, believing that the headteacher has not really taken account of their experience of the problem and does not have the parent's interests at heart.

This example also illustrates the third important consideration for staff wishing to use Restorative Interventions in schools: the issue of role clarity. As this issue applies to all Restorative Interventions, it will be considered in more detail in Chapter 7.

The next two subsections explore how children and adults can use mediation to address school-based conflict effectively.

Peer mediation

Peer mediation generally involves two trained mediators assisting fellow children who are in conflict to find their own way of resolving their problems.

Peer mediators offer a 'service' to their classmates, with 'cases' coming from informal self-referral and staff recommendation. The suggestion that children can be trained to operate as mediators, without the need for direct adult intervention in the conflict, usually generates some significant and legitimate anxieties among both staff and parents. Common questions that are raised include:

- Implementing peer mediation is a big undertaking for any school. What difference will having peer mediators make?
- Can children as young as 10 years old really learn to be effective mediators?
- Should peer mediators be involved in addressing incidents of bullying behaviour?
- Is it not asking too much of peer mediators if we expect them to intervene in other children's conflicts?
- How can we ensure that peer mediators do not get involved in situations that need adult intervention?
- Some parents may see the intervention of peer mediators as inadequate or as an abdication of the school's responsibilities. Will they not expect adult intervention and appropriate sanctions where children have behaved inappropriately?

We can explore the concept of peer mediation further by considering each of these questions in turn.

Implementing peer mediation is a big undertaking for any school. What difference will peer mediators make?
    The implementation of an effective peer mediation scheme requires:

- sound planning;
- understanding of the approach, and support from staff, parents and children;
- appropriate training for the peer mediators;
- ongoing adult support for the peer mediators.

In return for this investment, research suggests that effective peer mediation schemes can help the mediators and other children to learn how best to manage conflicts themselves, with less frequent recourse to adults. This results in fewer playground and classroom conflicts and so reduces the demands on staff to intervene in these conflicts. It may also equip the young people who experience mediation to better manage their conflicts in their adult lives, although this is harder to prove statistically.

Can children as young as 10 years old really learn to be mediators?

While some very young children can struggle to understand the concept of an impartial mediator, experience suggests that, with appropriate training, many children aged 10 and upwards will readily take to this role. In practice some children actually find it easier than some adults to take on the role of a genuine mediator. Perhaps this is because children have fewer and less entrenched learned responses to conflict, whereas some adults may need to 'unlearn' their entrenched attitudes if they are to become effective mediators.

Should peer mediators be involved in addressing incidents of bullying behaviour?

The short answer to this question is 'No'. This answer, however, assumes that the staff and children have a shared definition of what the school means by bullying. Some children may use the word 'bullying' to describe minor incidents that have led to friends falling out. It is important, therefore, that the peer mediators are alert to genuine bullying and are able to pass this on for staff to address.

Peer mediation may be described as an anti-bullying strategy, but only because it can help reduce some kinds of conflict that might otherwise develop into bullying. We explored in Chapter 4 how incidents involving significant harm create a moral imbalance between participants, why a response based on the mediation process is unlikely to be helpful and, more importantly, why it may place the person harmed at further risk. It would clearly not be appropriate to expect the person being bullied to make an equal contribution to 'the resolution of the problem'. It is also clearly inappropriate to ask young children to become involved in dealing with serious incidents that merit adult intervention. School staff may choose to use a Restorative Intervention to address bullying behaviour (see pp. 84–102).

Is it not asking too much of peer mediators if we expect them to intervene in other children's conflicts?

First, children do this anyway. There are some children who take on the role of 'peacemakers' in classrooms and playgrounds in any school. Peer mediation training can help them develop the skills and framework to do this effectively while providing legitimacy and support for their laudable pro-social activities.

Second, experience and research show that, with appropriate training and support, many children can take on this role without it becoming too much of a responsibility. Indeed, they can thrive on the responsibility and experience of working as part of a team.

Third, peer mediators always work in pairs. This helps to ensure that they feel supported, do not involve themselves in inappropriate conflicts and can easily seek adult help if required.

How can we ensure that peer mediators do not get involved in situations that really need adult intervention?

Part of the training and support process should aim to ensure that peer mediators know when they need to involve an adult. Typically, peer mediators will not be expected to mediate situations involving:

- adults;
- ongoing bullying behaviour;
- complex group dynamics;
- risk of personal harm to mediators or participants;
- incidents of significant rule breaking, lawbreaking or harm to others.

Peer mediation should normally take place in a private space, but close to adult help. Peer mediators should know who their adult support person is and how to contact them at short notice.

Some parents may see the intervention of peer mediators as an inadequate response or as an abdication of the school's responsibilities. Will they not expect adult intervention and appropriate sanctions where children have behaved inappropriately?

This concern is a strong argument for peer mediation being just one constituent part of the kind of whole-school approach to Restorative Practice that this book advocates. Where there is a distinctive difference between how children intervene in conflict and how staff deal with incidents, then parents are more likely to be confused about what approach the school is advocating. If children can learn to use mediation effectively, then so can adults. The school has a responsibility to inform and involve parents in understanding why Restorative Approaches are being adopted and how the children and school community each stand to benefit.

The notes in the following box highlight some of the key issues that schools need to consider if they are contemplating the introduction of peer mediation.

Establishing peer mediation: some key issues to consider

Planning

Effective planning and consultation are key elements in establishing a successful service in schools. Training providers should be able to advise during consultation on the following issues:

- Who, apart from children and teachers, do the school intend to involve in the planning, development and implementation of the scheme? Parents and non-teaching staff can have an important role to play.

• Does the school intend to promote it as a whole-school service or introduce it as a smaller-scale trial with particular year groups?

Choosing mediators

Who are to be the mediators? Possible selection criteria include age, personal skills, perceived position among peers, gender and ethnic balance, volunteers (elected or selected?), and distribution across teaching/year groups.

What about the need for parental involvement and permissions?

Training

Which staff should participate in the training? It makes sense to include one or more staff, teaching and non-teaching, in the training so that key staff are aware of the issues and can help the trainer address school-specific issues.

Timing of training sessions

The duration and timing of training depend on a number of issues, including the age and current skills of the selected children. A minimum of the equivalent of two full days' training (12 hours) is typical. It is also helpful to offer opportunities for brief follow-up training to reinforce learned skills and to offer ongoing support to those involved.

A 'dedicated service' or a 'generic skills' approach?

Is the emphasis to be on developing mediation skills in all children (perhaps eventually using your trained mediators as peer trainers) or on offering an 'expert' service that all children can be encouraged to use? These are not mutually exclusive approaches.

Access

How will children get access to the support of their mediators? This could be through formal self-referral (perhaps confidential, e.g. via postboxes), staff referrals, access through more open channels (e.g. requests arising from circle activities, playground approaches) or some combination of these.

Place in the current scheme of things

How will this service fit with other proactive and responsive approaches? How will it be reflected in relationship/behaviour/discipline and anti-bullying policies and procedures? What existing arrangements or procedures will need amended as a result?

Promoting, launching and maintaining the scheme

How can the school encourage children to take ownership of the programme? This is key to encouraging effective use of the service.

How will staff support the peer mediators on a regular and ongoing basis?

Adult mediation

The involvement of adult mediators in education is still a relatively new field. One recent example is the establishing of the parental right of access to impartial adult mediation services, enshrined for example within recent Scottish legislation – specifically, the Education (Additional Support for Learning) (Scotland) Act 2004. This lays a legal duty on each local authority to offer impartial mediation to parents who are in conflict with their local education service provider over educational provision for a child with additional support needs. Many successful mediation meetings have been held under this system, with parents and education services avoiding the need for more protracted and costly alternative dispute resolution procedures or litigation.

In practice there exist a complex range of conflicts in school communities in which it should be possible to offer mediation if there are sufficient trained facilitators available. These contexts are summarized in Table 6.2, with an indication of who might be best placed to offer the mediation.

In all mediations the participants are perceived as moral equals in the process, and the purpose is to help resolve a conflict and improve communication between the parties involved.

Table 6.2 Who should mediate?

Context for conflict	Who could mediate?
Child–child	Peer mediators or school staff
Child–staff	School staff or child and staff co-mediators
Staff–staff	Education service staff or independent mediators
Parent–school	Independent mediators (or perhaps education service staff)
Neighbour–school	Independent mediators (e.g. a local community mediation service)

Where, on the other hand, the overriding purpose of an intervention is to address a clear incidence of harm, the participants start from a different position – one of moral imbalance. In such a case, an appropriate Restorative Intervention will differ in a number of respects from the mediation process that I have described.

Restorative Interventions: the basics

Any Restorative Intervention that is based on the principles of Restorative Justice (see Chapter 2) aims primarily to address and repair the harm done by one person to another, or where two people have harmed each other. As with mediation, this is a voluntary process. However, in contrast to mediation, this kind of intervention can take place only when it becomes clear that a person who has caused harm accepts some responsibility for their actions. Importantly, this type of Restorative Intervention allows the *person harmed* to be involved directly in the outcome.

As we discussed in Chapter 2, the principles of Restorative Justice originated in indigenous communities in New Zealand and Canada, and have been shown in numerous studies to be effective in helping to address the needs of those responsible for causing harm (offenders) and those affected (victims). There is also mounting evidence that those offenders in the community who experience Restorative Justice are less likely to reoffend than those who experience only a punitive response.

Summary

The purpose of a Restorative Intervention is:

- to allow *the person harmed* to explain the impact of the harm on them;
- to allow *the person responsible for the harm* to understand the consequences of their behaviour for others and for themselves;
- to consider what *the person harmed* needs in order to help put things right;
- to consider what *the person responsible* could to do to 'put right' the harm done.

The primary focus is on addressing the harm done.

A genuine apology is normally part of the process, and a plan about future behaviours and supports will often be produced.

Relationships may be repaired or reconciled as a consequence, but this is not necessary to a successful outcome of the process.

There are examples of programmes in several countries where Restorative Justice is offered to young offenders to address relatively low-level, community-based crime. At the higher end of the offence scale, there have been well-documented cases of those who have committed offences as serious as murder being voluntarily brought together with the relatives of their victims in Restorative Interventions that have helped all concerned. In the United Kingdom, children and young people who have committed offences in the community are increasingly offered Restorative Justice as a means of involving them directly in addressing the harm they have done to individuals or to the wider community (e.g. by the Youth Justice Services in England and Wales and by Sacro in Scotland). Adult Restorative Justice services have also been established to help offenders and those who have been harmed (the victims) address the consequences of the offending behaviour.

In a school context, Restorative Justice processes have been adapted to allow trained staff to intervene where there are clear incidents of harm among children, between children and staff, and even between staff. At the low-tariff end of the scale this may involve a teacher having a brief Restorative Conversation with a child after a disruptive incident in the classroom. At the higher-tariff end of the scale this may involve a facilitator managing a Restorative Conference to address a serious incident of behaviour that could lead to a form of exclusion from school (see Figure 4.1). These conferences may involve one or more young people, their parents or carers and one or more members of staff. Two facilitators may be required to manage this process effectively.

Regardless of the seriousness of the incident, these types of Restorative Interventions follow an established theoretical framework that has evolved out of established practice and theory. This framework involves the facilitator in helping participants to explore:

1   *the facts*: hearing all participants' perspectives on what has happened, including perceptions of responsibility;
2   *the consequences*: understanding who has been affected and in what way;
3   *the future*: agreeing what can be done by the person(s) responsible to put things right, now and in the future.

This approach has been adapted in schools to provide a range of Restorative Interventions that can be tailored to suit the context. The most common examples of these interventions are:

• Restorative Conversations;
• Restorative Meetings;
• Restorative Circles;
• Restorative Conferences.

We shall consider each of these interventions in turn, with examples of suitable contexts for each. Before we do this, however, we need to consider the issue of voluntary participation. It is important to bear in mind that each of these Restorative Interventions can proceed only when at least one person is willing to accept some responsibility for harmful behaviour. At first glance this may seem to rule out a large number of incidents where we can expect the person who is responsible to deny any responsibility for their harmful behaviour. And yet, in the experience of those who offer Restorative Interventions in schools there is a much greater willingness among children and adults to accept responsibility for their own behaviours, compared with the responses under previous, more retributive approaches. It is worth considering what lies behind this shift in response.

The impact of harmful behaviour: encouraging personal responsibility

Making a genuine apology is an integral part of any Restorative Intervention. In Chapter 4 I asserted that a person responsible for causing harm is unlikely to be able to take responsibility for their harmful behaviour, or go on to make a genuine apology, unless their associated feelings of shame are managed appropriately. A Restorative Intervention offers those who feel unable to communicate their remorse spontaneously a structured opportunity and an emotional climate in which to manage their shame. The characteristics of this climate include:

- empathic, non-judgemental listening;
- a willingness to talk honestly about the consequences of the behaviour;
- support and affirmation when taking responsibility for the impact of behaviours;
- an opportunity to make a genuine apology that will not be dismissed.

If the facilitator of the intervention plans to bring the person harmed face to face with the person responsible for that harm in some form of meeting, then, in order to lay the basis for such a climate, there will need to be preparatory work done individually with the participants. The nature of this preparatory work will be explored later in the chapter. However, we will first consider a Restorative Intervention at its simplest, involving only two people in a dialogue.

Restorative Conversations

A Restorative Conversation is a dialogue that a member of staff can initiate with a child when either feels that the child has done something wrong. It is intended to help both participants address relatively low-level harmful or potentially harmful behaviours: disruptive incidents and minor misdemeanours. It is not intended for situations where one or more persons have caused significant harm to one or more other individuals. A Restorative Meeting, Circle or Conference might be appropriate in such a case.

Typically, a Restorative Conversation might last two to five minutes. It follows the 'facts – consequences – future' structure of all Restorative Interventions, and so the first task for the facilitator is to allow the child to describe, in their own terms, what happened. The child's response to this opening phase of the dialogue will determine whether it is appropriate to continue with the Restorative Conversation or whether some other action is required. Clearly, if the child, despite a supportive and skilled intervention, denies all responsibility for the misdemeanour, then a Restorative Conversation will not be appropriate. This may arise because the child in fact played no part in the misdemeanour, in which case the member of staff may need to act on any further information that they have heard from the child. Alternatively, the child knows that they did something wrong, but feels unable to own up to this in front of the member of staff. Whether or not a child feels able to accept responsibility for their behaviour will depend, in part, on how the facilitator approaches the first phase of the conversation – on how effectively the facilitator creates a climate in which the child can manage their own shame reactions.

The three hypothetical dialogues shown in Figures 6.2, 6.3 and 6.4 aim to demonstrate that the way in which we address a misdemeanour can have different purposes and can generate different outcomes. The (presumed) feelings, thoughts and actions of the participants are described in order to help explain what is happening and why the outcomes are different.

Clearly, only the third of these is a Restorative Conversation. It is the facilitator's skilful approach in helping the child to accept responsibility and manage her own feelings of shame that allows for a positive outcome.

The scenario is that a student is seen by the teacher to be texting on a mobile phone in class. The scenario is offered simply to illustrate the process. It may be that some staff would deal with this particular incident in a more low-key way. The purpose here is simply to illustrate how the process is managed and what it offers. As already stated, Figures 6.2–6.4 respectively show three different types of intervention.

Purpose: To establish blame/wrong-doing and impose a sanction.		
Teacher's feelings and words	**Student's thoughts and feelings**	**Student's actions**
(irritated) *Mary, what do you think you're doing?*	Feeling: *Anxious about pending confrontation. Shame at being caught.* Thinking: *Oh, no! He's seen what I was doing.*	Slips the phone into her pocket. *Nothing, sir!*
(Angry and exasperated) *What do you mean nothing? I saw exactly what you were doing. You were texting. You know the rules. Give me the phone!*	Feeling: *Defensive and embarrassed.* Thinking: *I can't afford to have my phone taken off me.*	*What phone? I don't have a phone!*
(Feeling frustrated and his authority threatened) *Don't have a phone? You must be the only one in the school, then! I saw you texting and I saw you put it in your pocket. Give it to me now or you're in serious trouble. You've already got yourself detention for this.*	Feeling: *Increasingly embarrassed in front of peers and anxious about likely outcome.* Thinking: *He can't force me to give it to him. He can't search me. Aggressive thoughts kick in.* Feeling: *Needing to control the situation.*	*No way! What are you going to do? Take it off me? Search my pockets? You better not lay a hand on me!*
(Losing his temper in the face of defiance. Shouting.) *How dare you threaten me! Get out of my room! Go to the headteacher's office right now!*	Feeling: *Under attack— overwhelmed and defeated. Losing her temper and out of control.* Thinking: *I'm in for it now. He's an idiot. He hates me. I hate him. I don't care what happens now.*	Jumps up, knocks desk over and storms out. *You can stuff your class. **** you!*
Duration: Approximately 50 seconds		
Outcomes: The situation is unresolved. Both are left feeling angry and stressed. Their relationship is damaged. A follow-up by headteacher will be required.		

Figure 6.2 Retributive blaming

Purpose:	To try to make the person feel bad or guilty about what they have done and to justify a sanction.		

Teacher's feelings and dialogue	Student's thoughts and feelings	Student's actions
Mary, what are you up to?	Thinking: *Oh, no! She's seen what I was doing.* Feeling: *Shame at being caught.*	Slips the phone into her pocket. *Nothing, miss!*
(Wearily, but trying to be reasonable and calm) Come on, Mary. I saw you with the phone. You know what the rules say.	Thinking: *I don't want to give up my phone. I need it today. I'll try to get on her good side.*	*Please, miss. I wasn't doing anything with it.*
Mary, I'm really disappointed in you. I could see you were texing.	Feeling: *Increasingly embarrassed and guilty.* Thinking: *Unsure how best to handle this.*	*I've put it away, now. I won't take it out again, Miss, I promise.*
That's not the point, Mary. You broke the rule and you know I have to confiscate the phone. Give it to me now, please.	Thinking: *She doesn't understand. I'm not going to get away with this.* Feeling: *Resentment and anger.*	*(Sullenly) On you go, then – take it. (Slams phone on desk) See if I care!*
You can collect it after school, assuming you lose that attitude first!		

Duration:	Approximately 40 seconds
Outcomes:	Mary's avoidance strategy (sounding reasonable, wheedling) failed. She resents having 'lost' and having to hand over her phone. She hasn't accepted any responsibility for what she did. Their working relationship has been damaged.

Figure 6.3 Retributive shaming

| Purpose: | To support Mary in taking reponsibility for what she has done, to allow her to make some reparation and to plan ahead. | | |

Teacher's feeling and language	Student's thoughts and feelings	Student's actions
Mary, can you put your phone away, please. I'll speak with you about it in a minute.	Thinking: *Oh. Oh! I've been caught.* Feeling: *Shame.*	Puts phone away.
A little later		
Can you tell me what happened there, Mary?		
	Thinking: *Where's this going?*	What do you mean?
Earlier on, when I asked you to put your phone away?		
	Feeling: *Shame and defensive.* Thinking: *I want to avoid dealing with this.*	Nothing much.
What was the 'nothing much'?		
	Thinking: *She knows, and she's not going over the top. I will risk being honest.*	OK. I was texting my mum, but I had to!
Thanks for being honest. You felt you had to text your mum?	Feeling: *Affirmed.* Thinking: *I need to explain/justify my actions.*	Yeah, 'cause I've arranged to go to Jean's after school and I realized she'll worry if I don't come straight home.
So it was important to let your mum know why you wouldn't be home. You didn't want her to worry.	Feeling: *Relief.* Thinking: *She seems to understand.*	Yeah, that's it.
So who has been affected by your texting in class?	Reflective thinking: *I haven't thought about that.* Feeling: *Shame.*	Well, me, I suppose, cause, I've got into trouble.
Were you affected at the time, when you were texting?	Reflective thinking:	I guess I wasn't paying attention to the lesson.
OK, so you've been affected quite a lot. Was anyone else affected?	Reflective thinking:	Well, you and the rest of the class, I guess.

Figure 6.4 A Restorative Conversation

How were we affected?	Reflective thinking:	You had to stop the lesson to deal with it?
That's true. How do you feel about it now?	Feeling: Shame and the need to be understood.	I wish I hadn't done it, but I really needed to let my mum know.
You really needed to let your mum know in class?	Feeling/thinking: Acceptance of responsibility.	No, I suppose I could have waited until later.
OK, so you wish you hadn't done it and you could have waited until later. Is there anything you want to do to put it right?	Feeling: Shame release.	I'm sorry. I know I shouldn't have done it.
Thank you, I accept your apology. What could you do in future if you feel you need to use your phone in class?	Thinking: Find a solution.	I could wait until break?
Waiting until break sounds like a good idea. Or, if it was really urgent, you could always ask me what to do. That way you wouldn't get into trouble. OK?	Feeling: Affirmed. I did the right thing by apologizing. I can deal with it better next time.	OK.
Thanks for that, Mary. I'm glad we sorted this out.		

Duration:	Approximately 120 seconds
Outcomes:	The situation has been resolved without great stress for the teacher. Mary has been helped to think meaningfully about what she did wrong and has made a geniune apology. Their relationship has not been damaged and has, perhaps, been strengthened. Mary has made a clear commitment regarding her future behaviour.

(Figure 6.4 continued)

This Restorative Conversation follows the format outlined in the next box, based on the 'facts – consequences – future' framework. The questions illustrate how the facilitator manages the process, but these questions are not scripted. Some Restorative Justice-based interventions are based on formally scripted frameworks but these can lack the flexibility of approach that is often required to meet the complex and varied contexts of relationships in schools. One of the skills of effective facilitation is in finding appropriate and responsive language that suits the context, without varying significantly from the principles or framework of the process.

Step 1. The facts: what happened?

E.g.   Can you tell me what happened?
I really want to know what you think happened there.
Could you tell me step by step what happened a moment ago/earlier today?
I want to hear what you have to say about it.
How did you feel at the time?

The facilitator summarizes the main points and affirms any accepting of responsibility by the child.

Step 2. The consequences

E.g.   Who has been affected by what you did?
How have you been affected?
Who else has been affected?
How do think they have been affected?
How do you feel now about what happened?

The facilitator summarizes the main points and affirms any understanding by the child of the impact of his or her behaviour.

Step 3. The future

E.g.   What do you think you need to do to put things right?
How can we try to make sure this doesn't happen again?
Is there anything I can do to help you achieve this?

The facilitator accepts any apology and summarizes any commitments, future plans or next steps that have been agreed.

Not every conversation will follow this clear and untroubled flow. A skilled facilitator will have a range of questions and responses that can be used to help the child stay focused on the purpose of the conversation and can help the child manage any of the 'fight' or 'flight' shame reactions that may arise during the course of the conversation (see Chapter 4). This need, to have knowledge and confidence in the process and access to a range of responses when conversations become difficult, can only be addressed through appropriate staff development and training – an issue to be considered in more detail in Chapter 7.

A Restorative Conversation can be an effective way of helping an individual to reflect on the impact of their behaviour. However, where the impact of that behaviour has caused significant harm to another individual or individuals, any intervention will be truly restorative only if those who have been harmed also have an opportunity to be involved in the process. Involving someone who has been harmed in a Restorative Intervention has two key purposes. These are:

1   to recognize and acknowledge that the needs of the person harmed are just as important as those of the person responsible for the harm;
2   to create an opportunity for the person responsible for the harm to hear directly from the person harmed about the impact of their behaviour.

Clearly, if the first of these purposes is to be fulfilled, then the participation of any person harmed will need to be voluntary. Equally, appropriate preparation will need to be offered to all participants if they are to feel safe and if the process is to meet the needs of all involved.

The simplest context for this type of intervention is where one person has caused harm to another, in which case a Restorative (face-to-face) Meeting can be offered.

Restorative (face-to-face) Meetings

The preparation stages and structure of a face-to-face meeting are outlined in Table 6.3. This outline assumes that the process involves one person responsible for causing harm and one person who has been harmed. Life is, of course, more complex than this. The process can be adjusted to accommodate other contexts – for instance where:

* Two individuals have harmed each other. In this case the preparation sessions would help both people to make apologies and appropriate reparation.
* The harm caused by one person has not specifically been to one other person (e.g. vandalism). In this case a representative of the harmed 'community' (e.g. the janitor or headteacher) could take the role of the person harmed.
* Two or more people have caused harm or been harmed. In this case the power dynamics may require more than one face-to-face meeting to be arranged, or the dynamics may be better managed through a Restorative Circle (see pp. 98–100).
* The person harmed does not wish to meet with the person responsible for the harm. In this case the person harmed may wish information about the impact of the harm to be conveyed by the facilitator to the person responsible. In practice, in most school contexts there is a willingness to meet, not least because it is likely that the participants will already have an ongoing relationship that needs to continue in spite of the harmful incident.

Table 6.3 Stages of a Restorative (face-to-face) Meeting

Stage 1: Facilitator meets with the person responsible

This stage involves first listening to the person's perceptions of what happened – the 'facts'. Typical questions will include:

- *Could you tell me what happened?*
- *What led up to that?*
- *What happened afterwards?*
- *Do you know what happened to the person harmed?*
- *How do you feel about what happened now?*

As well as building a rapport with the person responsible, this will allow the facilitator to establish to what degree the person is accepting responsibility for what happened and the appropriateness of proceeding with this type of intervention.

The facilitator will then establish how the person feels about meeting with the person harmed, will explain what the meeting process will involve and what opportunity there will be to give an apology and make amends.

Stage 2: Facilitator meets with the person harmed

This stage again involves listening to the person's perceptions of what happened – the 'facts'. Typical questions will include:

- *Could you tell me what happened?*
- *What led up to that?*
- *How has it affected you?*
- *How do you feel about what happened now?*

As well as building a rapport with the person responsible, this will allow the facilitator to establish any major inconsistencies between the participants' perceptions that may make a face-to-face meeting difficult. While there is no need for absolute concurrence on events, it is important that the basic facts and perceptions align.

The facilitator will then establish how the person feels about meeting with the person responsible. The facilitator will explain to the person harmed what the face-to-face meeting process will involve and what opportunity there will be to tell the other person how the incident has affected them and to say what they are looking for as an outcome of the meeting.

Stage 3: The face-to-face meeting

The facilitator will:

- agree ground rules for the meeting with the participants;
- explain again about the three stages of the process (facts: consequences: future).

Facts

- Invite the person responsible to describe and explain what happened.

(continued)

Table 6.3 continued

- Ask the person harmed whether they have any questions for the person responsible, or whether they would like to clarify anything from their perspective.

Consequences

- Invite the person harmed to say how they have been affected.
- Ask the person responsible whether they would like to respond, which includes their opportunity to apologize.
- Allow the person harmed to respond, if they wish.

Future

- Ask the person harmed whether they can suggest how things can be made right or how this kind of incident can be prevented.
- Ask the person responsible what they feel they can do to address these points.
- Ask if there is anything that the facilitator or other staff can do to help them keep to the agreement.
- Summarize the main positive outcomes from the meeting and thank them both for their participation.

Stage 4: Follow-Up

It may be necessary for the facilitator or another member of staff to follow up certain points or provide support in order for the terms of any agreement to be kept, according to circumstances.

Source: Adapted from *Restorative Practices in Schools: Manual for Facilitators*, Scottish Restorative Justice Consultancy and Training Service, Sacro (2005).

Whatever the scenario, the facilitator will generally meet first with the person who is apparently responsible for causing the harm. This allows the facilitator to establish the degree of responsibility being accepted by that person and their willingness to participate in a face-to-face meeting. Were the facilitator to approach the person harmed first, only to discover subsequently that the person responsible was unwilling to participate, this could leave the person harmed feeling aggrieved and dissatisfied with the intervention. The person responsible will also be asked to speak first at the face-to-face meeting (assuming there is only one). This gives them a chance to show their willingness to take responsibility from the outset.

The amount of the individual preparation and support required before the meeting will depend on individual circumstances. The amount of preparation may be quite limited where a Restorative Meeting is offered to address relatively minor incidents. Some schools have also used this process to deal with higher-tariff incidents, for instance as an alternative to formal exclusions, or as part of the 'return to school' process after exclusion. In such circumstances, significant preparation will be a necessary part of the process.

While the face-to-face meeting may prove beneficial for all participants, there will be instances where one or both participants will need additional support beyond the meeting. For example, the person responsible may request help with anger management; or the person harmed may need support to deal with future contact with the person responsible. These kinds of additional support may be identified during the future planning part of the restorative process, or may be more appropriately addressed on an individual basis outside the meeting.

The three following case studies help illustrate appropriate contexts for such face-to-face meetings and the different kinds of outcomes that can result. These are based on actual cases, although some information has been altered to maintain anonymity.

Case study I

This intervention involved a 13-year-old student diagnosed with Asperger's syndrome who experiences difficulty with social interactions and with selecting appropriate behaviours and responses. These difficulties were heightened by the boy's social development stage as he struggled to establish relationships, especially with the opposite sex.

The student's mother raised concerns with the school that he was being bullied by a girl in his class. The bullying had been happening on and off for months but was becoming more severe, with the girl concerned making fun of his speech and communication difficulties. When the school investigated the situation it became apparent that the boy, desperate to engage the girl in conversation, was being sexually inappropriate and the girl's reaction was to distance herself from him and to shun him, while still talking to his friends. Both children clearly felt harmed by the exchanges and agreed to a Restorative (face-to-face) Meeting. This proved to be helpful for a number of reasons:

- The boy was shocked when he heard how the girl was feeling when he spoke to her in the way he had used recently.
- The girl was upset to hear that all he really wanted to do was to be able to speak to her in the same way that his friends did.
- This process led to both children apologizing to one another and gaining an understanding of how the other was feeling.
- The boy went on to receive specialist support in pragmatic use of language linked to his age and stage that helped him to communicate more appropriately.
- The girl was subsequently able to say hello to the boy and pass the time of day with him without feeling afraid or vulnerable.

Case study 2

A 12-year-old boy had 'exploded' in class, swearing at the teacher and overturning a desk before storming out. The school decided to respond by offering a Restorative Meeting, and the facilitator established with the boy and the class teacher that they were willing to participate.

During the face-to-face meeting the boy was able to explain that he had just heard that he was going to have to move away from his mother's house and live with his separated father. The teacher's admonition for not bringing in his homework had been the tipping point for his anger. He accepted that his reaction was 'out of order' and listened while the teacher explained how she had been affected by his behaviour. The teacher was able to make some positive comments about the boy's usual behaviour in class and how surprised and scared she had been by his outburst.

In discussing how he could put things right, the boy offered to make a public apology in front of the class. The teacher felt this would be unnecessarily humiliating and said she was happy to accept a private apology, which he gave. He also agreed to help her with some tasks in the classroom at break time for the next three days.

Afterwards, both participants voiced their satisfaction with the process individually, with the teacher explaining that she valued the opportunity to hear his perceptions and to hear what she felt was a genuine apology.

Case study 3

Two 15-year-old boys were involved in a fight during school time inside the school premises. The fight had been organized via internet messaging and it was judged by the school to be extremely serious. The school felt the need to temporarily exclude both boys, and it was during the exclusion that the school made a request for an externally facilitated Restorative Intervention.

After a discussion of the incident with the deputy headteacher, it became apparent that two members of staff had been involved in trying to stop the fight and as a result had been affected or harmed by what had happened. These members of staff agreed to meet the facilitator to discuss how a Restorative Intervention could possibly help them. After some discussion, both staff felt that being able to tell the boys how their behaviour had affected them would be beneficial.

Meetings were arranged with the boys and their parents at home, and after the restorative process has been explained, the boys agreed to participate in a Restorative Conference. Both sets of parents also agreed to be involved. Both boys accepted full responsibility and expressed remorse for their behaviour. The conference was held at school, directly after the readmission meeting.

The meeting enabled the boys to face up to what they had done and, at the same time, to hear how their actions had affected others. They were also able to apologize genuinely and to give a commitment not to get into a similar situation in the future. The staff were able to ask the boys questions, tell them how they had been affected, and receive and accept their apologies. The staff members were also influential in deciding how amends were to be made. All involved expressed a high level of satisfaction via oral and written feedback received after the conference.

Restorative Conferences

For some incidents in schools it may be inappropriate for only the two people involved (the person responsible and person harmed) to participate in the Restorative Intervention. It may be judged valid and necessary to involve others such as parents or carers, or perhaps a staff supporter for a vulnerable member of staff. In this case a Restorative Conference could be appropriate. This may require two facilitators, as the degree of preparation and the dynamics involved in managing the face-to-face process may be significantly more complex.

Nonetheless, the nature of the preparation and the framework for the process will be very similar to that for a Restorative Meeting. Clearly, the time required of facilitators and of participants means that Restorative Conferences tend to be reserved for the most serious and most complex cases of harm. It may be that the school does not feel able to provide a facilitator for such a high-tariff intervention, or that access to a more independent facilitator may give the process the kind of gravitas that the situation merits.

Case study 3 illustrates a suitable context for a Restorative Conference.

Restorative Circles

Restorative Circles are distinct from the other circle processes described in Chapter 5 (community building, checking in, problem solving) because they follow the same structure and have the same purposes as Restorative Meetings and Conferences. The aim is to address a specific incident (e.g. vandalism, disruptive behaviour) that has created significant disruption or harm for all or part of a community – a group, class, year group or the whole school. As with Meetings and Conferences, all who will participate need to be prepared for the circle by the facilitator.

Restorative Circles should not be used for incidents that have caused significant harm to an identifiable person, such as group bullying of an individual. Face-to-face Meetings or Conferences would be more appropriate.

A Restorative Circle can be run as:

- a supportive process for all those affected by an incident or behaviour (i.e. where those responsible do not attend); or
- a way to enable people to take responsibility for their actions, find out how others were affected by what happened and come up with ways to avoid a recurrence.

It is important that the facilitator assess all potential participants to make sure they are suitable for a Restorative Circle and that they are appropriately prepared. This preparation will include checking whether potential participants want:

- to own up to and take responsibility for their part in what happened;
- to apologize for the harm they have caused;
- to make things right and try to stop it from happening again.

Or:

Table 6.4 Restorative Circle process

Facilitator	Opens the session, explains the purpose and structure of the process, helps the circle to agree ground rules.
Facts	
In turn, round the circle[a]	Each person says what happened and why.
Open forum	Anyone can ask questions or clarify facts.
Consequences	
In turn, round the circle	Each person says how he or she or others were (or might have been) affected.
Open forum	Anyone can say more about the consequences.
In turn, round the circle	Each person responds to what they've heard.
Future	
In turn, round the circle	Each person says how the harm could be addressed and this kind of incident prevented.
Open forum	Group discussion to evaluate the ideas, and come up with a final agreement or plan.
Facilitator	Writes up an action plan, reads it out to make sure everyone agrees, and asks all to sign, if appropriate.
Facilitator	Closes meeting.

Source: Adapted from *Restorative Practices in Schools: Manual for Facilitators*, Scottish Restorative Justice Consultancy and Training Service, Sacro (2005).

Note
a   As with all circle work, participants need not speak if they do not wish to.

- to get answers to questions;
- to say how they have been affected;
- to hear an apology;
- to have a say in how they can make sure it doesn't happen again.

Participants will need to be willing:

- to talk openly about their part in what happened;
- to think about how they will answer questions about their part;
- to reflect on and try to understand how others have been affected;
- to be willing to apologize for any role they played in causing harm;
- to make suggestions about what they could do to put things right and to help stop something similar from happening again.

If the participants seem able and willing, then a Restorative Circle can be held. A typical process for such a circle is outlined in Table 6.4.

The organization and running of such a circle are potentially time-consuming if appropriate preparation is to take place with all participants, and for serious or complex incidences of harm this will be necessary. However, in practice there is evidence that experienced school practitioners are able to build on existing circle approaches, such as problem-solving circles, and adapt these to deal with lower-level incidences with relative ease. If the children are already used to circle processes and are reasonably trusting of the facilitator, then the process can flow quite naturally from other circle work, with the facilitator being sensitive to individual vulnerabilities and adjusting the process accordingly.

There is evidence that these kinds of circles can be powerful ways of harnessing peer processes and can effectively pass ownership of the solutions to situations involving conflict and harm into the hands of those involved. Anxiety about the power available in such circles can also be a daunting barrier to school staff thinking of adopting this approach. This understandable concern highlights the need for appropriate training and support for staff adopting a range of Restorative Interventions.

Restorative Enquiry

A significant development in Restorative Practice in the United Kingdom in recent years has been the development of the concept of 'Restorative Enquiry' as a basis for introducing Restorative Practice in schools. This way of working restoratively has been developed by Belinda Hopkins, director of Transforming Conflict Ltd. The approach aims to apply aspects of both Mediation and Restorative Justice theory and practice in an adaptable process of open enquiry that enables staff and children to respond to incidents of conflict and harm appropriately.

Table 6.5 Restorative Interventions: guidance on when and where

Restorative Intervention	When?	Where?	Likely duration (including any preparation)
Conversation	As soon as possible, and at least on the same day.	Can be to one side of the class or group, if reasonably private, otherwise outside the class or at break time in an area that offers some privacy.	2–10 minutes.
Face-to-face meeting	The same day, if possible. Otherwise within a day or two.	In a private area or room, with no likely disturbance or interruptions.	15–60 minutes.
Circle	Can be planned in advance or offered spontaneously.	With a whole class in the classroom or with a smaller group in a room, where there will be no interruptions.	15–60 minutes.
Conference	Ideally, within a week of the original incident but may be longer.	Preparation work with supporters (e.g. parents) may take place in school or at home. The conference should be held in a private room, with no likely disturbance or interruptions.	Around 2 hours.

Detailed information on this approach is available elsewhere (see the 'Resources' section), and so we do not intend to explore the similarities and differences between this approach and those described in this book in any further detail here.

When, where and who?

One of the most common initial concerns that staff raise about Restorative Practice is the amount of time that might be required for the processes to be meaningful. Clearly, the Restorative Interventions described in this chapter need appropriate time to be effective. They also need to be conducted in a suitable place and at a time that is helpful. Participants are unlikely to 'buy in' to rushed processes or those offered in full public glare. Table 6.5 offers some guidance on these issues, although there may be good reasons at times to vary from this. The amount of preparation required with individuals will determine the overall duration of the process. Generally, the time spent on preparation increases with the complexity or seriousness of the situation.

It would be unwise, and potentially unsafe, to facilitate an intervention if the participants are not emotionally ready for it. For instance, they may be too angry or too upset to contribute effectively. An important function of any preparation with individuals will be to gauge these issues and plan the timing of the intervention. In high-tariff cases, participants may need other kinds of individual support to help them get to a point where they can participate meaningfully in a Restorative Intervention, as will be discussed.

Time is not elastic. When choosing to offer Restorative Interventions, we have to make judgements about the best use of time. However, our consideration should not be restricted to a judgement about the amount of time that the process itself will take. There is good evidence that the consistent use of such interventions pays dividends in terms of more pro-social behaviours and a reduction in incidents in the future. Restorative Approaches not only are effective at the time, but are an investment. We need to be willing to make that investment if we are looking for meaningful changes in the longer term.

In practice, schools have proved to be creative and resourceful in finding ways to ensure that staff and children have time to work together effectively.

Who should offer any given Restorative Intervention?

Ideally, the member of staff who is present at the time of the concern should offer a Restorative Conversation, provided they have had appropriate training and can make the time available to have the conversation. When another adult has to intervene to offer the conversation, we risk disempowering the member of staff who is most directly involved in the relationship with the child.

With Restorative Circles it may be appropriate for the class teacher to facilitate the process. Certainly all staff who are involved in the issue being considered should be part of the circle. However, there may be times when it is helpful for a different adult to facilitate the process, particularly if the class teacher is feeling harmed.

A member of staff who has been affected by an incident or who is clearly part of the 'solution' should not facilitate Restorative Meetings and Conferences. As with formal Mediation, it is important in this context that the facilitator is perceived by the participants to be as impartial as possible. Once more, this is an issue of *perception* rather than *intention*, and so there may be a small number of cases where the school will want to invite a genuinely impartial third party to facilitate the process. There are a growing number of agencies that have staff trained in these approaches. Increased emphasis on multi-agency collaboration and 'joined up' working should make this kind of service easier to call on in the future. In Scotland, schools are now able to access local restorative youth justice services, such as Sacro, to deliver this type of intervention. Indeed, the process mirrors very closely the type of Restorative Conference that youth justice services can offer in offender-based contexts.

Other supportive interventions

Before a Restorative Intervention takes place, other action may need to be taken. This will usually be for reasons of:

- safety – it may be necessary to separate individuals to ensure their own and others' safety;
- emotional security – participants may need time or support to manage their emotions before becoming involved in the process; or
- access – time may be required to arrange for parents to be involved or to access independent facilitators.

It is important that these kinds of actions are not perceived as sanctions by the participants if the subsequent Restorative Intervention is to be as effective as it can be.

Example

A child can experience the practice of being removed from class because of disruptive behaviour as a sanction – when it is 'done to' them. However, many schools operate 'time out' systems that are genuinely negotiated with the children and staff, to ensure that all parties' immediate needs are being met. Here the 'time out' experience can be a supportive one for the child and can be a precursor to a Restorative Intervention.

Despite the sophisticated range of Restorative Interventions that exist, it is clear that these alone cannot always address every individual's needs. There are other supportive interventions that appropriately trained professionals can offer that do not involve bringing people face to face to address conflict or harm. Each has its own process and purpose. Some of the more common examples include:

- counselling-type interventions (e.g. person-centred; solution-focused brief therapy; cognitive behavioural programmes);
- 'victim awareness' programmes;
- 'support for person harmed' programmes;
- various group support programmes.

It is not unusual for schools to identify that a person involved in a Restorative Intervention may need one or other of these supportive interventions as well. This need may be identified as a result of initiating a Restorative Intervention, and any subsequent additional support may run in addition to the restorative process.

These forms of support can be extremely effective when offered appropriately but it is beyond the scope of this book to consider them in any detail. Further information about some of them can be found via the 'Resources' section.

Deciding which response is appropriate

Mediation and Restorative Interventions are the two most common Restorative Approaches adopted by schools when addressing conflict and harm respectively. (Table 6.7 at the end of this chapter summarizes the main differences between these two approaches.) Other types interventions have also been mentioned. This diversity of options raises a key question: *How can staff make meaningful and safe decisions regarding which response is appropriate?*

This is a relatively new question, even for those schools that already use responsive approaches, as awareness and understanding of the full range of distinctive approaches described in this chapter are still developing. So far I have been reviewing and explaining existing and established practice. What follows is a new framework that is offered as a model for the decision-making process when staff want to intervene restoratively.

An assessment and decision-making process

Any decision making by a member of staff regarding how best to intervene is essentially an assessment process. This assessment can be broken down into four distinct stages: 1) Gathering information and perceptions; 2) identifying needs; 3) selecting due process; 4) safety and participation. The information in Table 6.6 summarizes what is going on in each of these stages.

Breaking the assessment process down into four stages like this may seem to suggest that it is necessarily a laborious and time-consuming process. In practice, particularly for low-tariff interventions, staff can do all of this in the few minutes it takes to speak with individuals prior to a meeting. The stories may be short and simple, and the needs of the individuals clear, so that the choice of process is obvious and participants may already be familiar with that process and so need less preparation.

More thorough and careful assessment will be necessary in higher-tariff incidents as it is in these cases that by offering prematurely an inappropriate intervention, we risk escalating rather than resolving a conflict. Worse still, we may end up further harming someone who has already been significantly harmed.

A skilled restorative practitioner working to bring people together within this practice framework will choose and adapt their approach in order to ensure that the needs of the participants are met appropriately. This will involve facilitating a climate that is conducive to apology and reparation,

Table 6.6 A four-stage assessment and decision-making process

Information and perceptions
This stage is about assessing the situation with those involved, often individually. It includes:

1 Hearing the stories.
2 Working with participants to decide who should be involved.
3 Checking the perceptions and feelings of the parties, including establishing:

   • Was anyone harmed?
   • Does anyone accept responsibility for causing harm?

Identifying Needs
This stage involves helping the participants to articulate their needs and interests. What are they looking for? What are their priorities? Do these involve:

1 addressing harm or wrongdoing, through apology or reparation;
2 resolving conflict, through mutual agreement;
3 repairing relationships and improving communication?

Selecting due process
This stage requires the person who is intervening to decide what form of intervention would be most appropriate, based on its purpose and its ability to meet the participants' needs. Questions to consider include:

• What response options are available (e.g. Mediation, a Restorative Intervention, counselling, group support programmes, etc.)?
• Which best meets the needs of those involved?
• Do I have the skills and knowledge to offer this intervention myself?
• If not, who is best placed to offer the intervention?

Note: In some situations, more than one need may exist, in which case the intervention will aim initially to address the most pressing need.

Participation and safety
This stage involves ensuring that there is informed consent to take part and that participants are not unduly at risk physically or emotionally.

• Do the parties understand the process that is being offered?
• Are the parties willing to take part?
• Will anyone be put at significant risk by the process?

and/or supportive of mutual agreement about future behaviours, according to participants' needs. All responsive approaches will create opportunities for more constructive communication and improved understanding between those involved.

Where, after assessment, it is judged that *any* of the following pertain, then some form of individual support will be more appropriate than face-to-face interactions.

- The presenting need is primarily for individual support.
- Any participant will be put at significant risk by the bringing of participants together.
- Any participant does not wish to meet with the others involved or affected.

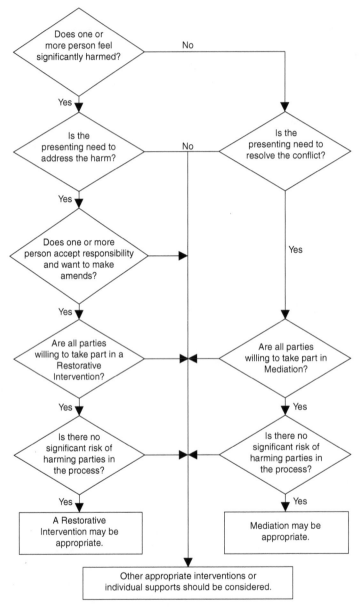

Figure 6.5 What kind of Intervention: A decision tree

The 'decision tree' shown in Figure 6.5 can help to guide you through these stages. This need not be as mechanistic a process as the diagram might imply. Staff will need to use their judgement to respond sensitively to individual circumstances.

Table 6.7 Summary of the key differences between Mediation and Restorative Interventions

	Mediation	Restorative Interventions
Primary Purpose: What is the primary purpose of the intervention, in terms of establishing constructive communication, resolving conflict and/or addressing harm?	The primary purpose is to resolve a conflict by reaching a mutually acceptable agreement and/or increased mutual understanding.	The primary purpose is to address the harm resulting from particular behaviours by addressing the needs of both the person harmed and the person responsible for the harm.
Prerequisite conditions: Other than informed consent and agreement to work to predetermined ground rules, what prerequisite conditions need to exist if a face-to-face meeting is to be appropriate?	Participants need to have expressed a desire to work towards a mutually acceptable agreement/ understanding.	One or more participants needs to be accepting responsibility for having caused harm to another participant and needs to be prepared to apologize and possibly to make reparation to the person harmed.
Moral compass: What role does the process play in reflecting any moral judgements made by the school community about the relevant behaviours of the participants?	None. The process is not based on any moral assumptions about participants' contributing behaviours. Participants are free to reach separate conclusions about the morality of their own and other participants' behaviours.	There is a shared understanding among participants and facilitators at the start of the face-to-face meeting that the person responsible has caused harm, that the harmful behaviour was morally wrong and that the person harmed has a right to an apology.
Anticipated outcomes: What outcomes are anticipated (as opposed to guaranteed) when participants agree to take part in a face-to-face meeting?	A mutually generated acceptable agreement that resolves the conflict and/or increases mutual understanding. More constructive communication in the future is a common, but not presumed, outcome.	The person responsible will make an apology to the person harmed. Other reparation and commitments regarding future behaviours may also be agreed. More constructive communication in the future is a common, but not presumed, outcome.

Chapter 7

Implications for individual staff

O wad some power the giftie gie us,
To see ourselves as others see us!'
(Robert Burns, 'To a Louse')

Restorative Approaches are more likely to succeed if they are implemented by staff who share the fundamental values and beliefs that underpin restorative thinking and interventions. People do not learn to be effective restorative practitioners from books alone.

This chapter considers:

Familiarity with the ingredients does not a cake make
How restorative is your thinking?
Modelling
Facilitating Restorative Interventions
Role clarity and the role of other Restorative Practice agencies
Initial training and ongoing development

Familiarity with ingredients does not a cake make

You may have read this book and found many of the ideas in accord with your own thinking. Alternatively, these ideas may appear new, challenging and even strange. You may have recognized elements of the various approaches that already exist in your own practice, or these may be quite alien to you. To learn to be effective practitioners we need to develop three areas of self that inform who we are, regardless of our starting point in the learning process (Figure 7.1):

- *Behaviours*: We need to consider how we behave towards others, and how we develop the restorative responses we use in our work.

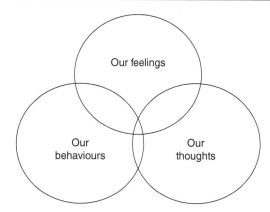

Figure 7.1 Three aspects of self

- *Thoughts*: We need to examine our understanding of the ideas and processes that constitute Restorative Practice, as well as what we think about those we work with.
- *Feelings*: We need to explore how we feel about responding restoratively rather than retributively. We need to consider how we manage our feelings when we work in emotionally demanding ways.

We also need to have regard for three component parts of Restorative Practice itself; that is, not just for the restorative *processes* we use but, equally importantly, for their associated *skills* and underpinning *values*. These component parts are co-dependent and hierarchical – see Figure 7.2.

In other words, we cannot implement effective processes without having appropriate skills to do so. Equally, the skills and processes in themselves are unlikely to have a restorative impact unless they are delivered from a genuinely restorative value base.

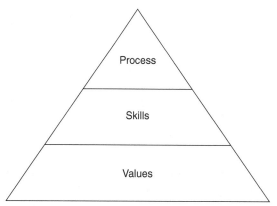

Figure 7.2 The component parts of Restorative Practice

This chapter aims to help you to reflect on some of these key areas. However, people do not learn to be effective restorative practitioners from books alone, so we will also consider the key issues in relation to the kind of training that staff need.

In any group of twenty staff that I introduce to Restorative Practice there will regularly be at least one who says, 'I'm doing this already!' For me this is good news, if the statement is absolutely accurate. However, when someone expresses this perception it makes me doubly sensitive to the issue of what staff *think* Restorative Approaches are compared with what they *look and feel like* in practice. It is not uncommon for staff who go on to take part in experiential training to say that, while they had recognized parts of what was said, or had thought they had a firmly restorative value base, on closer examination they had discovered challenges and ways of working that they had not considered before. (Hence the title of this section.)

Teaching is a peculiar profession. The climate of professional individualism that has persisted for many years, and that still exists to a degree in most schools, encourages us to develop and then become dependent on a raft of individually learned behaviours and responses to conflict and harm, often learned in isolation. These 'keep us afloat' in our day-to-day interactions. We need to reflect upon and may need to unlearn some of these if we are to be genuinely effective in our restorative practice. This process can be surprisingly demanding for some staff. Nonetheless, if we genuinely believe that the children we work with can change their ways of thinking and their behaviours when offered a conducive climate, then presumably we believe the same of the adults who wish to create that climate.

How restorative is your thinking?

In Chapter 3 we looked at the values underpinning all Restorative Practice. The activities in Figures 7.3, 7.4 and 7.5 are designed to help you to reflect on how closely your current values and beliefs match these. You can use this exercise on your own or you can use and discuss it with a group of colleagues. What matters is that you are honest in your responses, not that you try to match up to some notional ideal.

Note: If you choose to share and discuss you responses with colleagues, it may be helpful to agree beforehand that each person's opinion is valid and that any debate or disagreement will be handled respectfully.

Retributive thinking has been part of our culture for hundreds of years and is still embedded in most school responses to harm and wrongdoing. You may well have experienced this retributive culture when you were a pupil. It would not be surprising if you rated yourself quite low on a number of the statements in these exercises. Although retributive thinking permeates many aspects of our society, it is clearly a learned way of thinking; we are

Look at each statement about children and young people. For what proportion of children do you believe each statement to be true?						
1 = none 2 = very few 3 = less than half 4 = more than half 5 = almost all 6 = all children						
Beliefs	**1**	**2**	**3**	**4**	**5**	**6**
Children are social creatures – they prefer to feel they belong rather than to feel isolated or rejected.						
Children can develop a sense of fairness, justice, right and wrong.						
Children change, and their behaviour can change.						
The way I work with and relate to a child can influence his/her feelings, thoughts and actions.						
Reflection/discussion point						
For any beliefs that you have indicated do not apply to all children, why do you believe this to be the case?						

Figure 7.3 Beliefs about children

Indicate how strongly you hold each of these values.			
1 = not at all 2 = moderately 3 = strongly			
Values	**1**	**2**	**3**
I respect each person's rights, regardless of what I think of his or her behaviour.			
We should each take responsibility for our own behaviours.			
Those involved most closely in any conflict or harm, including those harmed, should have the greatest say in the outcomes of any intervention.			
When someone has done something wrong, they deserve opportunities and support to put things right.			
Reflection/discussion point			
What specific conditions or circumstances might test your adherence to those values that you hold most strongly?			

Figure 7.4 Core values

Scenario 1: Imagine you have discovered that something you did or said has inadvertently caused someone else real offence or harm and you are now being held accountable for this by someone in a senior management position. In this context, how strongly do you agree or disagree with the following statements?

1 = disagree strongly 2 = disagree 3 = unsure 4 = agree 5 = agree strongly

Response	1	2	3	4	5
People in conflict should be helped to find their own solutions rather than be told what to do by authority figures.					
Punishing people who have done wrong tends to compound their problems rather than help them change their behaviours.					
It is important that someone who has caused harm has an opportunity to explain his or her actions.					
Someone who has caused harm should be given an opportunity to make a genuine apology.					
It is important that someone who has caused harm has an opportunity to hear how their behaviour has affected others.					
A genuine apology should be recognized as a significant step forward for the person making the apology.					
Restorative responses are more likely to help people change their behaviour than retributive ones.					

Turning the tables

Scenario 2: Now imagine that you, or someone you care about, has been harmed by someone else in an incident, e.g. a theft or mugging. Re-read the statements and note whether your level of agreement has changed for any of them. The higher you rate yourself for each statement in either scenario, the closer you align yourself to Restorative values and beliefs. Any shift in your responses between the two scenarios may reflect a difference in what you *think* about Restorative Approaches compared with how you *feel* about them.

Figure 7.5 How do you currently respond to conflict or harm?

not born with a 'retributive' gene. As with all learned ways of thinking, it can be unlearned when a valid and more positive alternative is available. This is a matter of personal choice.

Of course, we are each entitled to hold to our views and values, wherever these lie in the retributive–restorative continuum. It is unlikely that you would want to introduce Restorative Practice into your way of working if you did not hold restorative values and beliefs. You certainly should not feel compelled to do so. Many staff who have experienced effective staff development and training have reported that the process of questioning and reflecting on these values has helped them identify more strongly with restorative values. Learning to use Restorative Approaches will allow you to put these values into practice in skilled and consistent ways. Perhaps the most powerful experience of all is having an opportunity to participate in a well-run Restorative Process for real, as a person harmed or in conflict or as a person responsible for causing harm.

Modelling

> If we are not modelling what we teach, then we are teaching something else.
>
> (Helen Flanagan)

In Chapter 3 we considered the significance of those attitudes and behaviours that adults model for children in schools in their day-to-day interactions and relationships. Any consideration of modelling raises a key question: *How can we know whether we are modelling the kinds of attitudes and behaviours that are associated with Restorative Practice?*

The evidence that will help us answer this question can come from two distinct sources (see Figure 7.6). These sources are interdependent, with each informing the other.

Self-awareness

Self-awareness in this context means your ability to monitor and evaluate your own attitudes and behaviours, and your awareness of the impact that these have on others. This is an essential, if sometimes fickle, source that you need to draw on in order to develop your restorative practice. As a starting point, you can use the open questions from Tables 7.1, 7.2 and 7.3 to help you reflect on some key attitudes and behaviours that you would expect to be modelling when promoting constructive communication, resolving conflict and addressing harm.

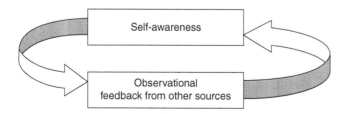

Figure 7.6 Information sources about modelling

Table 7.1 Promoting constructive communication: reflective questionnaire

- What kind of communication skills and attitudes do I want the children I work with to learn from me?
- How frequently do I ask for a child's perspective?
- How willing am I to listen to and to value a child's perspective, either when I ask for it or when it is offered spontaneously?
- Specifically, in what ways do I demonstrate that I value a child's perspective?
- How frequently do I interrupt a child when they are trying to tell me something, and why?
- What balance do I strike between asking open and closed questions?
- To what degree am I able to feel empathy for each child I work with?
- Specifically, how do I communicate the empathy that I do feel?
- How else do I show respect for each child?
- How do children know how I feel?
- How do I communicate what I am happy about?
- How do I communicate what I am not happy about?
- When I choose not to communicate my feelings genuinely (honestly), why do I do this?

Table 7.2 Resolving conflict: reflective questionnaire

- How do I want the children I work with to react when they are involved in conflict?
- How frequently do I raise my voice, and why?
- How do I react when conflict arises between two children?
- Do I encourage them to take responsibility for resolving their conflict? If so, how?
- What criteria do I use for deciding when I need to intervene in a child–child conflict?
- When I do intervene, how engaged do the children remain in finding a resolution?
- How do I react when conflict arises between a child and me?
- When I am in conflict with a child, what part does the child play in resolving the conflict?
- How do I feel about children being aware of and observing adult–adult conflict?

Table 7.3 Addressing Harm: reflective questionnaire

- How do I want children to respond when they have caused harm and when they have been harmed?
- In what ways do I acknowledge that people may be feeling harmed after an incident?
- When someone is feeling harmed, how do I support them in addressing the harm done?
- What opportunities do I offer the person responsible for the harm to put things right?
- How easy do I find it to accept some else's genuine apology for harm that they have caused me?
- How willing am I to acknowledge the fact when I may have caused someone else to feel harmed?
- How willing am I to apologize to others, including children, when I become aware that I have caused them feelings of harm?

Observational feedback from other sources

We might like to think that we can accurately assess our own attitudes and behaviours but ultimately it is the feedback that we get from others that provides us with much of our source material for this self-assessment. After all, it is not so much our *intentions* in behaving in certain ways towards others as their individual *experiences and perceptions of our behaviours towards them* that will influence their responses.

> The messages we send others are not always the same as the signals they receive.

And so, each person with whom we interact provides us with a mirror, albeit a somewhat distorting mirror, for us to learn about the attitudes and behaviours that we model for the children in our schools.

Observational feedback can come in a number of forms:

Unsought feedback

We pick up people's responses to our behaviours through our day-to-day interactions with them. Our awareness of others' responses may at times be quite low, and at other times may be heightened by circumstance. Nonetheless, this type of feedback is constantly influencing our own perceptions and so contributes to our developing self-awareness. Paying attention to this kind of feedback can pay dividends for our working relationships.

> ## Example
>
> I worked for a while supporting a child who was finding maths particularly difficult. I became increasingly frustrated as he struggled and failed to grasp what appeared to me to be a simple aspect of multiplication. The more I tried to explain how to do the multiplication, the more he struggled and the more frustrated we both became. We were going nowhere. Finally I realized that my frustration was partly a reflection of his *own* sense of frustration. Instead of trying to 'teach' him how to 'do it properly', I changed to asking him to explain how he was working it out. As he struggled to articulate the various steps he was going though, and as I visibly worked to understand his perspective, he became more relaxed about the problem. I too became less frustrated and progress became easier.

Sought feedback

We can also explicitly ask others for feedback about the attitudes and behaviours that we model. One way this can be done is through structured experiential exercises, for example practising a particular process and getting feedback from the other participants and/or from an experienced observer. This type of feedback should be an integral part of any staff training in Restorative Practice.

We can also obtain feedback through observation of our interactions with pupils by colleagues, mentors, inspectors, etc. Some school staff can find the mere thought of such observational feedback quite daunting. To be meaningful for the individual, any such observational feedback should, ideally, be managed in a voluntary and non-threatening way. The aim should be to make observations within and at the fringes of the individual's 'comfort zone'. The person being observed should decide along with the observer those aspects of their behaviour and attitude on which feedback is being sought.

Option

In this context, the reflective questions on constructive communication, resolving conflict and addressing harm (Tables 7.1–7.3) could form the basis of a peer observation exercise.

Perhaps a less threatening, if still potentially daunting, source of feedback involves viewing a video of your own practice. Clearly, there are ethical issues regarding permissions to be considered here. Where such an exercise can be arranged, the experience can be an extremely enlightening one, although it is perhaps best undertaken as part of a staff development programme where a supportive colleague can provide 'impartial' comment on the video, in order to counterbalance any tendency for you to be overly self-critical!

Third, and perhaps most importantly, we can seek feedback directly from the children we work with. They are in some respects best placed to give us relevant feedback, since it is they who experience the attitudes and behaviours that we model. This again is a potentially threatening area in which to tread. However, if approached appropriately and with sensitivity, the children with whom we work can provide us with rich reflective material. In recent years, increasing numbers of teachers have found ways of seeking feedback on issues such as lesson content and homework. Asking children about their experience of how we as staff relate to them is equally feasible.

Finally, we need to be wary of the potential pitfall in believing that modelling is a one-way process – only something we do in order to influence others. The last reflective question for this section is: *How open am I to changing my own attitudes and behaviours in the light of the attitudes and behaviours that others model for me?*

Role clarity and the role of other Restorative Practice agencies

It is possible to integrate Restorative Practice so that it permeates many aspects of our daily interactions. The modelling of pro-social behaviour by adults will nurture pro-social behaviour among children. There are, however, some significant implications for staff who wish to facilitate higher-tariff restorative interventions in relation to the role that they are adopting.

Consider a situation where a senior member of staff plans to facilitate a face-to-face meeting between a child and a teacher in response to an incident in which the child has behaved inappropriately towards the teacher. There are a number of issues that need to be considered:

- How able is the senior member of staff to take an unbiased role in facilitating the process?
- Will he or she be able and willing to respond appropriately if it emerges that the teacher has contributed to the child's behaviour through some unskilled, ill-advised or inappropriate adult behaviour?
- How will the participants (i.e. the child and the teacher) perceive the senior staff member's role in the process? If the child believes that 'staff always back each other up', then the child is unlikely to invest genuinely in the process. If the teacher already has a poor working relationship with the senior member of staff, this too will influence participation.

There are clear advantages to schools building their internal capacity to manage restorative responses rather than relying on external staff and agencies to facilitate interventions. However, in certain situations there may be reasons why it would be more appropriate to make use of external facilitators. The advantages of each option are summarized in Table 7.4.

As we move towards greater inter-agency cooperation, it seems likely that schools will want to engage with external restorative services, such as youth justice services, where these exist locally. It seems equally appropriate that access to these services will be reserved for the highest-tariff or most complex situations. More commonly, school staff will choose to intervene directly. When staff do offer Restorative Interventions, they need to be clear about the distinctive role of the facilitator and need to communicate what that role is, in order to avoid role confusion and wrong assumptions on the part of the participants.

Table 7.4 Advantages of internal and external facilitation of Restorative Interventions

Internal facilitator	External facilitator
Increased ownership of the process and solution	A greater likelihood that participants will perceive the facilitator as impartial
A deeper understanding of the contexts and of any wider issues in any incident	Facilitators from external restorative services may well have greater skill levels and experience of facilitating
The ability to follow through in supporting the outcomes of any agreement or plan	Avoids excessive demands being placed on school staff to manage more complex and time-consuming cases
The possibility of a prompt response to a concern or incident	External agencies may be able to offer dual facilitation with school staff in appropriate cases.

Facilitating Restorative Interventions

As a member of staff intervening in an interpersonal conflict, is it reasonable to expect that you can 'repair' the relationship?

The restoration of any relationship is ultimately in the control of those who constitute that relationship. For you to actively *repair* other people's relationships implies a mechanistic process that is inconsistent with the values of a Restorative Approach. The process of repair can only be *done with* people's willing participation, not *done to* them. In a Restorative Approach your aim is to help create, or facilitate, a climate in which those involved in a damaged relationship can *choose* to address harm done, in order to resolve conflict and to improve communications.

So, for a Restorative Approach to be effective, it needs to be facilitated rather than imposed or 'taught'. Learning to facilitate requires specific skills and understanding. As a way of interacting it is quite different from the didactic teaching methods that many of us experienced as pupils and perhaps practise now in school. In a didactic approach to teaching, you know what you want people to do or to learn. Your job is to get them to that point – in other words, you aim to manage the *outcome*. As a facilitator, your aim is to manage the *process*. An analogy may help.

An analogy

Imagine you are a driving instructor. For each lesson, you decide the route and destination for your learner driver. Your job is to teach the skills and knowledge that the learner needs to be a safe driver and to pass their driving test.

One day, on the way to collect a learner you arrive at a junction controlled by traffic lights – but today the lights are not working. There is chaos and, to prevent accidents, you jump out of the car and take on the job of managing the flow of traffic. You have now chosen to become a *facilitator* of traffic flow.

This may appear a simple enough task. But without a sound understanding of what you are trying to achieve, and without appropriate communication skills and the confidence to use these, things may go horribly wrong. Your aim is to manage how many vehicles you let pass, at what speed and from what direction. Your job as a facilitator is to help people get to where *they want to go* by managing the traffic flow safely.

Imagine how drivers will react if you revert to 'instructor mode'. They will not appreciate it if you stop them in order to tell them what you think their destination should be, and what you think of their driving. They may become resentful and choose to ignore you. They will react even more strongly if you climb in, push them aside and attempt to drive them to where *you* think they *should be* going.

You will know you are doing a good job as a facilitator when people are moving on to their destinations with a minimum of distraction, diversion or disruption.

Facilitation, then, is not about determining the outcomes for the participants. It is about managing a process – its ebb and flow. It is as much about knowing *when not to* intervene as it is about applying skilful intervention.

Typically, in a restorative process the participants will speak for 80 per cent of the time and the facilitator for 20 per cent.

For those of us who have grown up and practised our work in a more didactic teaching culture, this way of working requires something of a leap of faith – to begin to believe that we can allow others to find their own directions and to support them in reaching their preferred destinations best by helping to 'manage the flow'.

The shift to a facilitative way of working can be both daunting and liberating: daunting because it involves giving up any learned need to direct, or even control, the outcome – where *you* want people to end up; liberating because you can allow participants to take responsibility for their own outcomes while you focus your efforts on *effective communication* and *management of the process*.

This is why learning to use Restorative Approaches generally requires specific experiential training. Most people who work in education will already have a range of helpful skills that can be built on and brought into conscious use when facilitating. Some staff will already adopt a facilitative approach in some aspects of their work. After all, facilitation is not a new concept. The

Taoist philosopher Lao Tse (sixth century BC) wrote, 'To lead people, walk beside them.... When the best leader's work is done the people say, "We did it ourselves!"' Perhaps facilitation is also a leadership style?

Initial training and ongoing development

Some of the skills inherent in Restorative Practice, such as communication, empathy and facilitation, are common to other aspects of teaching and work with children generally. However, it is worth stating at the outset that training in Restorative Practice will not help staff to address problems that they are experiencing if they have poor conflict resolution or poor classroom management skills. There is an assumption in much Restorative Practice training that staff are already able to manage their conflict and teaching at a professionally satisfactory level. If these are areas of weakness for an individual teacher, then it is advisable for them to seek specific training to address these aspects before embarking on Restorative Practice training.

I have already emphasized that this book cannot be a substitute for the kind of experiential learning that is involved in professional development and training in Restorative Approaches. Effective support in developing Restorative Practice will ideally include all of the following components:

- *Awareness-raising sessions.* As well as outlining what Restorative Approaches look like in practice, these sessions will also explore why Restorative Approaches will have greater impact if embedded in a compatible, whole-school approach to relationships. There will be opportunities for staff to reflect on and discuss their values and beliefs in relation to Restorative Practice. There will also be opportunities to consider the implications of Restorative Practice implementation and contribute to the planning process.

- *Initial training in Restorative Interventions* These sessions will help staff to reflect on and consciously develop the interpersonal skills that are inherent in Restorative Approaches, including active listening, appropriate questioning, assertiveness and facilitation skills. Staff will learn the details and language of the processes and will practise managing these processes through role play and other exercises, with individual feedback from colleagues and experienced trainers.

- *Ongoing development and support.* Staff will, at the least, have opportunities to meet with colleagues on a regular basis to share experiences and engage in further practise sessions. Ideally, trainers will provide support on a regular basis, with top-up training offered as necessary. For those learning to facilitate in higher-tariff situations, there will be opportunities to shadow and co-facilitate interventions led by more experienced practitioners.

It is unrealistic to predetermine exactly what level of training individual staff will need. This will be determined by the skill levels of the staff, the intended pace of implementation and the quality of training on offer. However, Table 7.5 gives some guidance on the likely duration of awareness-raising and training, based on practical experience. The table is based on a cumulative training model; in other words, participants would progress through the sessions from the start-up to the point appropriate to their needs. These timings are offered for general guidance. In practice, training sessions should be tailored to individual and organizational needs.

In Chapter 6 I described a range of distinctive approaches to responsive intervention including Mediation, Restorative Enquiry and Restorative Interventions – each with different purposes and process frameworks. If these processes are useful to schools and are appropriate to different contexts, then this raises a simple question: *In order to have access to an adequate range of responses, do schools need to train their staff in all the processes?*

Learning to be an effective mediator, or learning to facilitate a Restorative Conference, in other community contexts (such as community mediation or restorative youth justice) typically requires a high level of initial training – typically five days' attendance, plus associated reading – followed by opportunities to co-facilitate, ongoing professional support, assessment and supervision. Does this mean that teachers will need training in all of these approaches to implement Restorative Practice safely and effectively?

In practice this has not been my experience. Schools are learning to adapt these processes to meet their needs and those of the participants. There are a number of facts and factors that need to be considered when planning staff development programmes:

- Many of the skills and qualities needed to be an effective mediator or facilitator of restorative interventions are shared (e.g. active listening, questioning, facilitation and process management), and so staff who have received in-depth training in one approach are unlikely to need full training in the other.
- Not all staff will need the same level of training. Staff will start with different levels of skill and understanding. Some will have had training in relevant core skills via other pathways.

Table 7.5 Typical duration of training sessions

Session	Approximate duration
Introductory awareness-raising	2 hours
In-depth awareness raising	0.5–2 days
Initial training in low-tariff interventions (day-to-day classroom or playground incidents)	3–6 hours
Initial training in face-to-face meetings	1–2 days
Initial training in circles and conferences	1–2 days

- All staff may wish to be able to manage a Restorative Conversation or simple Restorative Circles, or to use basic mediation skills, but it is unlikely that all will need to (or have time to) facilitate more complex face-to-face meetings or conferences.
- Regardless of the expertise of individual staff, there will always be a place for 'outside' organizations to provide independent Mediation or Restorative Justice services for higher-tariff and complex cases.

The introduction of a whole-school approach to Restorative Practice will, for most staff and schools, be a significant and evolving journey. Identifying appropriate training to suit both the needs of staff and the pace of change is one of the major challenges for school management and education service staff. A sample school development programme will be considered in more detail in Chapter 8.

Training and ongoing support have been shown to be vital components of effective Restorative Practice development in schools. If we are too quick to label practice as 'restorative', without taking time to examine that practice and measure it against that of experienced practitioners, then at best we risk diluting the quality of what we offer. At worst, we risk harming those whom we invite to be involved in our interventions.

If you ever work with an experienced restorative practitioner – and I hope you get the chance – they will tell you that Restorative Practice is not a destination; it is a journey in itself. In travelling that road we can learn as much from those we work with as from those who offer us training. At its most rewarding, it can become not just a way of working, but a way of relating to others – in essence, a *way of being*. Just as the development of children's emotional intelligence is fundamental to effective learning, so the development of our own emotional intelligence is fundamental to effective teaching.

Chapter 8

Implications for schools and education services

This chapter considers:

> A background to 'behaviour management' in schools
> Restorative Practice and behavioural approaches
> School readiness and self-evaluation
> Whole-school implementation: what might it look like?
> Developing policy and practice
> Restorative Approaches: a self-evaluation toolkit for schools

A background to 'behaviour management' in schools

The management of child behaviour has long exercised schools. Concerns about attitude, application to work tasks and general social behaviour can be traced back to the origins of compulsory education and the establishment of schools. This concern perhaps reveals much about the extent to which the way we have structured education in industrialized society is compatible with and takes account of the psychological development of children and young people. It is noticeable that each generation of educators would appear to observe a detrimental decline in behaviour and attitude. Some prefer to reflect on a previous age when children were apparently well behaved and respectful of authority. Evidence suggests, however, that the management of child behaviour has always tested the resources of teachers and encouraged a search for strategies and solutions.

The concern of teachers with managing behaviour is not an end in itself; rather, it is essential to enable schools to function as organizations and communities. It contributes to the personal and social development curriculum, but also, and perhaps most importantly, it is a cornerstone of effective learning and teaching.

Schools are complex social organizations and as such require systems, structures and rules to enable them to function effectively. At one level these are purely operational, and apply to all organizations – for example, in using accommodation and allocating staff to tasks. However, there is also a need to have systems and processes in place to regulate social interaction in a way that enables people to coexist harmoniously, and act together to achieve certain outcomes. Where schools differ from many organizations, of course, is the extent to which all the participants within the system share the same focus: learning and teaching. As a result, the ability to manage differing understandings of aims and purposes becomes a key task and is a critical factor in the overall effective functioning of the organization.

The latter part of the twentieth century saw the development of personal and social education as a key element of the school curriculum. This reflected a recognition of the critical structural role that schools have always played in conveying widely held social values and mores. However, it also relates to the perception of significant change in key social institutions such as the family, and a consequent need to explicitly support children's social, emotional and personal development as effectively as possible. The management of behaviour in schools contributed to this process. Thus, schools began to address behavioural concerns and issues explicitly, with a view to enabling children to develop a set of pro-social behaviours that would serve them well in wider society.

The latter part of the twentieth century also saw a growth in the understanding and application of the psychology of learning, and this was reflected in the development of curricula, technique and practice, and resources. Underpinning this was a growing understanding of what made for effective classrooms, and in particular the significance of effective child management. In Scotland this led in 2000 to the publication of *Better Behaviour, Better Learning*, a seminal Scottish government report that recognized the complex interaction between learning and behaviour in schools. This encouraged the development of a range of initiatives, of which Restorative Practice was one.

Of course, *Better Behaviour, Better Learning* reflected work that had been continuing in Scotland and elsewhere over a number of years (see Chapter 2), but it served to draw this work together and clearly emphasized that in order to achieve better learning outcomes, teachers had to become more effective in how they engaged and supported the individual learner and managed the classroom setting. The task for education services and schools therefore became the development of policies and practice that would enable this to happen. *Better Behaviour, Better Learning* also served as a marker for the journey that many education services find themselves on now, moving from policies and practice with an emphasis on 'discipline' through 'behaviour management' to 'relationships', reflecting an acknowledgement that human relationships are at the heart of everything that schools do. This shift acknowledges the inherent paradox in the notion of 'managing' a child's behaviour and recognizes the ultimate goal of enabling all young people to become effective managers of their own behaviour.

Restorative Practice and behavioural approaches

There are inherent and inevitable tensions between approaches to behaviour in school that are based on restorative principles and those based on behavioural theory. The development of Restorative Practice in Scotland since 2004 is offered here as a useful illustration of how Restorative Approaches can develop in schools where the recently prevailing approach to 'behaviour management' has been based primarily on behaviourist approaches.

The *Better Behaviour, Better Learning* report (2002) led to a number of initiatives in Scotland, including the development of Restorative Practice in educational settings. Although prior to the publication of the report there was some evidence of such activity in Scottish schools, it was piecemeal and practice based, with little apparent in terms of coherent, underpinning theory. The national Restorative Practice initiative gave the educational community an opportunity to consider how such theory and practice could be adapted to serve the needs of schools, and to learn from the experiences of educational settings in England and elsewhere, where such development had already begun. The remainder of this section and the next describe and explore how one education service has approached this change process, and explores some of the resultant learning.

In this education service a small group comprising education service management, schools' representatives, the continuing professional development team and the psychological service was established to take forward a number of themes, including the governmental Restorative Practice pilot initiative, which involved three Scottish education services. In this particular authority, six schools were invited to participate in the Restorative Practice pilot, and a pilot schools steering group was established.

This group quickly identified two issues.

First, as they learned more about Restorative Practice, they realized that its success would rest fundamentally on the beliefs, values and ethos of their schools, and not just on the practice. Indeed, they believed that the application of the practice in a setting where the ethos was unsupportive or incompatible would lead inevitably to its failure, and ultimately to its rejection. It was therefore agreed that the initiative would be known as 'Restorative Approaches', and that its development would support schools to reflect on and understand their underlying value systems regarding their approach to child behaviour before developing systems and practice. As one headteacher said, 'It's much more than practice; it's a way of being.' This aspect of implementation will be addressed in more detail later in this chapter.

The second issue that schools identified concerned the compatibility of Restorative Approaches with behavioural approaches to managing behaviour. Recent years have seen a significant growth in the application of approaches to child and classroom management which have their roots in behavioural psychology. In simplest terms, these approaches reflect theoretical principles that behaviour which is rewarded will occur more, and behaviour which is ignored or punished will decline. In the 1960s and 1970s, behavioural programmes moved from laboratories into more naturalistic settings, and their application became more widespread. In schools, teachers found they had access to potentially powerful behaviour control and management tools, and the 1980s saw a growth in the development of a range of techniques aimed at developing the teacher's capacity to manage the classroom by managing the consequences of children's behaviour in systematic and consistent way.

Teachers consistently evaluated such behaviourally based approaches as helpful, as they offered a clear and reasonably simple approach to managing complex situations and were relatively easy to learn and develop. Teachers reported significant reductions in their experience of stress, associated with a greater sense of control in the classroom. However, critiques of such approaches have emerged over time, and it is relevant to explore these in the context of developing management approaches based on restorative principles. In Chapter 4 we considered why sanctions are less effective than Restorative Approaches in developing pro-social behaviours. However, there is no doubt that some aspects of behavioural approaches offer positive and effective strategies. These can be summarized as follows:

- *Recognition of the importance of teacher behaviour.* Central to all behavioural approaches is the principle that what the teacher *does* makes a difference in the classroom. Effective and successful teacher behaviour is described and methods of analyzing behaviour and style are offered. Effective classroom management is seen to involve a set of skills that can be learned. While this may seem self-evident, it is often the perception of teachers who are experiencing management difficulties that whatever they do makes little or no difference in the classroom. This principle fundamentally challenges that.
- *Catching children being good.* Research clearly demonstrates that in classroom settings, teachers are more likely to attempt to manage behaviour by picking up on negative or unacceptable behaviour. In contrast to responses by teachers to academic behaviour, social behaviour is much more likely to elicit criticism than praise. Behavioural approaches encourage teachers to identify and respond to the behaviour that they want in their classroom and, in doing so, draw attention to positive models and ensure a more balanced distribution of attention to children in the classroom.
- *Being clear about expectations.* Behavioural approaches emphasize the need to be explicit about what rules or expectations apply in a classroom. They do not assume that everyone will know what appropriate behaviour is and do not rely on children breaking rules to find out what limits are. Setting rules also offers an opportunity for children to engage in the process of setting expectations for their own behaviour.

Research indicates that people are more likely to follow rules if they have had some involvement in their establishment rather than having them imposed.

• *Acceptable behaviour can be taught.* Following from the previous point, behavioural approaches encourage explicit teaching of what constitutes acceptable behaviour, and offer a variety of techniques to support children in developing the repertoire of behaviours that will facilitate learning and social interaction.

• *Behaviour is a choice.* Behavioural approaches promote the idea that we all make choices about how we behave, and that with practice and support we can make good rather than bad choices. Children are encouraged to anticipate the consequences of their behaviour and choose behaviour that is socially acceptable and appropriate rather than behaviour that breaks rules or fails to meet certain standards.

• *Consistency is important.* Behavioural approaches aim to establish consistent teacher behaviour so that responses to behaviour are, as far as possible, invariable and predictable. They also encourage the adoption of consistent approaches across a whole school to ensure consistency between different adults when dealing with children.

• *Behaviour management is fair.* Finally, if behaviour management systems are explicit and consistent, they are more likely to be seen by children as fair. Less time and energy will be spent on disputing the teacher's response to unacceptable behaviour if it is seen to be just and predictable.

So, in what ways are behavioural approaches incompatible with restorative approaches? Criticisms fall into four main areas:

1   A fundamental aim of any system that addresses behaviour is to develop in the child the capacity, and the desire, to manage their own behaviour and behave in socially acceptable ways when they are independent of adults. Indeed, some behavioural approaches strongly assert the belief that children whose behaviour is effectively managed through such a system will behave appropriately in settings where the behavioural contingency system does not operate. However, there is a genuine concern among some practitioners that being subject to external systems of control can actually make a child or young person less likely to behave appropriately in the absence of such external influence. The key question to be asked is: *To what extent does a given approach enable a child to develop a genuine understanding of their own behaviour and responses in various situations, and to internalize both the desire and the capacity to behave in a socially acceptable manner?*

Restorative approaches have at their core a belief that to achieve genuine growth and development, children and young people need to be supported in understanding the nature of their behaviour and its consequences, and that this can rarely be done by using simple behavioural 'operant contingency' systems.

2   Human behaviour, especially in social interactions, is complex; inevitably, the task of managing such behaviour is also complex. While increasing consistency and reducing unpredictability is undoubtedly a desirable goal in effectively managing behaviour, it is unrealistic to suggest that responding to situations can be done in a mechanical, fixed way. We need to be able to manage situations flexibly, while operating within clear limits, ensuring as far as possible that all concerned can understand why certain responses are made at certain times.

3   A key criticism of behavioural approaches is that they fail to acknowledge the social and emotional relationship that exists between teachers and children. Yet we know that the quality of relationship can be a key factor in how effectively teachers teach and children learn – and behave. Failing to recognize the subtle yet powerful interaction that takes place, and its associated emotional components, can both reduce the capacity for change and growth and fail to build on a potential key strength.

4   For some children, behaviour is not always a choice. Ylvislaker and Feeney (1998), writing from a psycho-neurological perspective, advises that 'An impulse is not a choice.' It is perhaps disingenuous to suggest that we should always consider a child's behaviour to reflect a choice they have actively made, and respond accordingly. Our task is surely to identify when it is not a choice and support the child or young person in recognizing that fact for themselves, and in working towards exerting greater self-regulation. A restorative model, based around genuine conversation and linked to effective self-regulation strategies, is much more likely to achieve this. A behavioural approach, which does not offer the opportunity to do this, is unlikely to enable a child or young person to internalize the knowledge and control required for real development.

Evolution and transition

Given how well established behavioural approaches are in some schools, it will not be realistic, possible or even desirable to ask staff to abandon their use of these strategies and techniques. Initially the challenge may be to recognize the useful practice and techniques that behavioural approaches already offer, but also to recognize their limitations, and to consider how Restorative Practice may be judiciously introduced to gain maximum benefit in developing children's capacity to manage their own behaviour in a socially acceptable manner.

Evidence suggests that schools which introduce Restorative Approaches effectively can dramatically reduce their reliance on behavioural approaches. Schools and education services that wish to introduce Restorative Practice will need to consider to what degree a shift away from reliance on behavioural approaches is an explicit aim or simply a gradual consequence of implementation. (The place of sanctions is considered in Chapter 4.)

School readiness and self-evaluation

In developing Restorative Approaches, the education service became aware that there was evidence of aspects of restorative practice already in existence in its schools (e.g. peer mediation). However, there was no overall coherent theoretical perspective underpinning this. Such practice would appear to have developed in a naturalistic and random way. It was also clear that for some schools the adoption of Restorative Approaches would represent a significant departure from existing behaviour management models and present a real challenge to prevailing attitudes and behaviours. There was concern that in these circumstances, attempting to adopt a Restorative Approach, without having created the conditions in which it could flourish, could lead to failure and ultimately rejection. For these reasons, a school readiness self-evaluation tool was developed that would enable schools to evaluate their position relative to the key principles of Restorative Approaches.

Research indicated little previous work in this field – surprising, perhaps, in view of the challenge that introducing a radical model such as Restorative Approaches could pose in some school settings. From the work of Van Ness and Strong (2002), a simple self-evaluation toolkit that explores four factors critical to success was developed. The toolkit is designed to support schools in identifying potential development activities to be undertaken in advance of embarking on actually developing a restorative model. Of course, in some cases schools will be ready to begin developing such a model, but the toolkit can still be valuable in clarifying with school staff what will be involved, and how Restorative Approaches will fit with both the practice and the ethos of the school.

A copy of the toolkit and introductory guidance notes is given at the end of this chapter (see pp. 141–146).

Central to the successful adoption of a restorative model is the principle that all members of the organization or community need to have a sense of involvement in the development of the approach, and that there should be some broad and commonly held values within the organization that are consistent with a restorative perspective.

Outlined on the following pages are the four key factors that the toolkit explores and related key themes that schools are invited to address. Schools are encouraged to adapt the toolkit and to use it in a way that best fits their needs. Some schools have used the questions as the basis for discussion groups while others have used it as a staff survey, collating returns in advance of a joint staff development activity. Some schools have used the toolkit to compare pre- and post-development views. However it is applied, there is strong encouragement for schools to use it as a development tool and map out activities that they can undertake as part of their adoption of Restorative Approaches. Schools are also invited to identify other information that would contribute to an evaluation of the organization's openness to the cultural and relational change that embarking on the 'restorative journey' can require.

The key factors that the toolkit explores are as follows:

- *Factor 1: Meetings, communication, agreements.* These processes are central to Restorative Approaches, and while schools will be very familiar with all of them, there is a need to explore in some detail how staff understand them, and how skilled they feel in their application.
- *Factor 2: Apologies, reparation, behaviour change.* A fundamental principle of Restorative Approaches centres on the benefits of offering genuine, sincere apologies for harmful behaviour and, where appropriate, undertaking some form of reparation. Additionally, the belief that children and young people can change their behaviour is a cornerstone of the approach.
- *Factor 3: Social integration.* Human beings are social animals, and seek relationships and involvement with others. Responses to unacceptable behaviour sometimes involve the social exclusion of those who have misbehaved. A restorative perspective suggests that this approach rarely brings about effective long-term change in behaviour, and is more likely to be counter-productive.
- *Factor 4: Whole-school involvement.* Schools are complex organizations in which issues like relationships and behaviour have a widespread impact on a day-to-day basis, as well as the development of ethos or culture. The value of consistency of policy *and* practice across schools in key areas, such as behaviour management, is now well understood, as is the contribution that everyone has to make in developing these.

In addition to these four factors in the toolkit, schools will also need to consider the degree to which they already embrace the kinds of proactive approaches that will underpin effective Restorative Practice. The questions in the box below highlight the key areas.

Most schools are unlikely to achieve unanimity among their staff when using school-readiness toolkits and questionnaires, but the process of discussion and debate that these tools can generate will form an important part of the development process. However, the greater the diversity of responses among the staff of a school, the more preparatory work probably needs to be done with staff. This work would aim to address the basic

---

Proactive approaches

1   In what ways does the school's curriculum explicitly teach effective communication and conflict resolution skills?
2   What opportunities are students and staff given in school to share their concerns and feelings about relationships (student–student and student–staff)?
3   What structured opportunities exist for students to offer each other support (e.g. peer support programmes such as buddying, peer mediation, etc.)?
4   How *effectively* and *consistently* do staff individually model the kinds of values, attitudes and behaviours that you want your students to learn and to demonstrate in their own relationships?
5   What continuing professional development (CPD) opportunities already exist to support staff in developing effective interpersonal skills?

---

values and principles of Restorative Approaches, in advance of staff training or implementation of specific practices.

A more detailed, reflective questionnaire on how the school currently responds to serious incidences of conflict and harm is given in Figure 8.1.

Whole-school implementation: what might it look like?

Research and experience to date suggest that there is no universal template for the implementation of Restorative Practice that can be successfully applied to all schools. And yet it is not unusual for schools that are considering embarking on the process to ask what implementation might specifically look like as a planned process. This section offers a sample development model, many components of which you could expect to see in any school's plans. However, this should not be treated as the only model. Schools need to pay heed to their own development needs and will often find individual and creative solutions to meet these needs.

What follows on pages 133–37 is a description of a model over three phases covering respectively the short, medium and long term. The duration of each of these phases will depend on a number of factors, including:

•   school readiness;
•   effective planning processes;
•   prioritizing of resources, including staff time;
•   school size;
•   staff turnover rates;
•   access to quality training and support.

The following questions will help the school as a whole to reflect on how closely current responses to conflict and harm are aligned to the thinking behind Restorative Interventions.	
When an incident happens: How does your school support communication between those involved to attempt to resolve the issue?	Response:
People harmed	
How does your school give support to, and respect, those who have been harmed? To what degree does your school give all those harmed a chance to express their views and feelings?	
People responsible for causing harm	
To what degree does your school give those responsible for causing harm a chance to express their views and feelings? What kind of support does your school give them? Does your school give them a chance to apologize and/or make amends?	
Overall	
To what degree do all those affected by an incident have a say in the outcomes? How aware of Restorative Approaches are your staff? How much does your school already encourage the use of Restorative Approaches? How Restorative are your existing relationship/behaviour/discipline policies?	

Figure 8.1 Whole-school responsive approaches: questionnaire

Overly rapid implementation is likely to lead to low levels of ownership and poorly integrated skills and processes. An unnecessarily drawn out implementation programme is likely to result in a loss of momentum and direction. Larger schools will typically be working to a three- to five-year development programme.

The short term

All staff

All teaching and other staff will participate in awareness-raising sessions that will encourage reflection and discussion in the following areas:

- understanding the underpinning values of Restorative Practice;
- considering the advantages and implications of a shift from a retributive to a restorative culture;
- understanding what Restorative Practice looks like when in operation;
- understanding the implications for the individual and for the school community of implementation, including necessary training and support commitments.

'Early adopters' will participate in a voluntary CPD programme offering training in constructive communication and conflict resolution skills, including Restorative Enquiry/Language/Conversations. Voluntary support group(s) will meet on a regular basis to reflect on and share experiences and to provide mutual support. Where possible, the group will be supported by relevant 'external' agency staff (see below).

Key staff

In addition to participation in the above, all members of the senior management team and a selection of relevant key staff (e.g. child support, pastoral care, faculty heads) will participate in in-depth training to allow them to:

- assess the need for higher-tariff interventions;
- use mediation skills;
- manage Restorative (face-to-face) Meetings;
- refer the most serious cases on to outside agencies (where available).

Key staff will have opportunities to shadow or co-facilitate Restorative Interventions. Staff who deliver health and well-being programmes will be trained to introduce constructive communication and conflict resolution skills to the health and well-being programme in a phased development, where these do not already exist.

Students

All students will participate in introductory sessions on Restorative Practice that will encourage reflection and discussion on the following areas:

- understanding the underpinning values of Restorative Practice;
- considering the advantages and implications of a shift from a retributive to a restorative culture;
- understanding what Restorative Practice looks like when in operation and their role in it.

Learning how to use constructive communication and conflict resolution skills will be phased in as part of the health and well-being programme. Any existing peer support programmes will be consolidated. Students will be offered an opportunity to further develop peer support programmes, including a peer mediation service. Initial training will be undertaken.

Parents/carers

All parents will be offered awareness-raising sessions that will encourage reflection and discussion in the following areas:

- understanding the underpinning values of Restorative Practice;
- considering the advantages and implications of a shift from a retributive to a restorative culture;
- understanding what Restorative Practice looks like in practice and their potential role in it.

Information (leaflets, the school website) will be made available and circulated to all parents on the above.

Support agencies/organizations

Training providers (external and/or education service based) will deliver training to support the developments above. Relevant agencies that can provide other Restorative Interventions (e.g. the police, social services, local community mediation services) will develop or consolidate appropriate links with the school community. This process may include opportunities to offer joint interventions. Relevant agencies will take referrals to intervene where it is not appropriate for school staff to do so.

The medium term

All staff

'Top-up' sessions will be offered to reinforce the original content of awareness-raising input. New and newly qualified staff will participate in awareness-raising sessions as part of their induction process. Information on expectations and available support will be made available to all supply and temporary staff.

Through a rolling programme, all staff will have access to CPD in constructive communication and conflict resolution skills, including how to manage a Restorative Conversation. Early initiators will have access to CPD in managing Restorative Circles for classes and groups.

Key staff

Key staff will have access to CPD in managing Restorative Circles for classes and groups. Key staff will shadow, co-facilitate or refer on appropriately those Mediations and Restorative Interventions that they feel unable to manage alone.

New key staff will have access to relevant CPD. All staff who deliver health and well-being will teach constructive communication and conflict resolution skills within the health and well-being programme.

Students

All students will be able to learn constructive communication and conflict resolution skills as part of the health and well-being programme. Recently introduced peer support programmes will be consolidated. Selected students will be trained as peer mediators and supported in establishing a service.

Parents/carers

Parents will have opportunities to participate as supporters to their children in Restorative Conferences, as needs arise.

Demand for parent sessions on Restorative Approaches to parenting will be gauged and sessions trialled.

Support agencies/organizations

Relevant agencies, including training providers, will support all of the above and will provide support and supervision to school staff who are delivering Restorative Interventions on their own.

The long term

All staff

Ongoing top-up sessions will continue for new staff. All staff will be using constructive communication, conflict resolution skills and Restorative Conversations as part of their everyday interactions.

All relevant staff will have access to CPD in managing Restorative Circles for classes and groups.

Key staff

Key staff will be using mediation skills and Restorative Interventions (Meetings and Circles) to address the vast majority of concerns 'in-house'. Only the highest-tariff cases and those that require an entirely neutral facilitator will be referred on to appropriate agencies.

Students

All students will continue to develop and use their constructive communication and conflict resolution skills. Students will manage peer support programmes, including peer mediation, with appropriate support from relevant staff.

Parents/carers

Parents will continue to participate in Mediations and Restorative Interventions, as appropriate. They will have the option of using their learned skills with their children at home.

Support agencies/organizations

Relevant agencies will:

- provide support and supervision to school staff who are delivering Mediation and Restorative Interventions on their own;
- take and manage a relatively small number of referrals for Mediation, Restorative Conferencing and other support interventions.

Developing policy and practice

The experience of piloting the introduction of Restorative Approaches has led to a number of conclusions about the factors that contribute to successful implementation. These conclusions are supported by evidence from a number of evaluations, and include the following.

The education service has to commit

The management team of the education service must signal clear, public support for the implementation of Restorative Approaches, and this commitment needs to be demonstrated in contacts with schools. Wherever possible, education service management-led policy and guidance should reflect Restorative Approaches, not least in terms of language. An expectation that a restorative perspective will underpin the resolution and management of all behaviour and relationship issues should be cultivated. Managers of the service need to consider to what extent their own practices are restorative, especially in the area of grievance and conflict resolution. Restorative practice is much more likely to develop in individual schools if they are part of a broader culture that supports, and to some extent demands, such an approach.

The support and involvement of school managers is critical

In a similar way, within a school it is vital that managers give genuine, consistent support to developing Restorative Approaches. This requires them to be familiar with both theory and practice, and to demonstrate this in their dealings with children, parents and staff. All senior management staff should undergo a significant level of training. To be effective, a Restorative Approach cannot be switched on and off. It needs to be embedded in the culture of the organization and should inform all aspects of the interactions which take place. This does not mean that managers must take all responsibility for leading such a development, but it does mean that their support of it needs to be unequivocal and visible.

Schools need to be ready

Schools need to be ready before they undertake the development of Restorative Approaches. They need to explore honestly and rigorously the attitudes that inform existing practice, establish consensus as far as possible regarding the direction in which they wish to move, and identify steps to be taken to make this happen. Some schools might have to recognize that they are not ready to begin the process of developing Restorative Approaches, for example if staff views are fundamentally divided or if the school has other major development priorities. In such cases there is little sense in pressing forward with an initiative that has little or no chance of success.

Schools need a plan for the 'journey', including parental involvement

I would encourage schools to map out their likely journey before they start on the development of Restorative Approaches, and to anticipate the challenges they may encounter on the way. In doing so, they are more likely to develop workable solutions that will be efficient in terms of time and resources. A key area to consider is parental involvement. For many parents, Restorative Approaches present a challenge to their own experiences and expectations. Early attempts to publicize and explain the approach will go some way towards helping parents understand the approach and feel more able to support its application. In some cases, schools have gone beyond this and have offered parents support in developing their own ability to use a restorative model in managing children's behaviour.

Quality training matters

For Restorative Approaches to be genuinely embedded in school practice, staff need skilled support in order to help them:

- understand the underpinning value base and to challenge some learned attitudes and behaviours;
- develop their interpersonal skills and apply these appropriately;
- learn to manage specific restorative processes.

The quality of implementation of Restorative Approaches will depend on many factors, but a lack of appropriate training will undoubtedly lead to ineffective practice. Schools and education services are increasingly looking to sustainable development models based on the use of 'in-house' trainers. Restorative Practice remains a relatively new development area within most education services and so they may not have access to sufficiently knowledgeable and skilled 'internal' trainers of their own. There is an increasing if limited pool of recognized and experienced independent trainers who can provide direct training and help to build organizational capacity, for example through 'training for trainers' programmes. The field of Restorative Practice training is not regulated, and formal accreditation systems are still rare. Those engaging external trainers should ask some pertinent questions, including:

- What experience do the trainers themselves have of using Restorative Approaches with children?
- What restorative model or specific interventions are they able to provide training in?
- What experience and qualifications do they have as trainers?
- How sound is their knowledge of the application of Restorative Approaches in school settings?

No one size fits all

There is no one standard approach that suits all schools, though there is of course a clear, universal underpinning philosophy that needs to be adhered to. The ways in which this philosophy is applied reflect the natural organizational and cultural differences between schools, and can lead to a rich variety of practice. The task for strategic developers at school and education service level is therefore to ensure that schools can effectively comply with a set of principles, not to impose a particular practice template.

Make sure it all fits together

Internal consistency of both values and practice is essential when developing Restorative Approaches. Schools therefore have to ensure that the restorative perspective is not undermined by systems that are incompatible, for example by using a retributive response to a certain type of unacceptable behaviour. Inevitably such double standards will devalue the integrity and effectiveness of a restorative model. This applies also, and perhaps particularly, to the management of relationships between adults within a school. To be truly effective, Restorative Practice needs to inform all aspects of social interaction within the community; it should not stop when we enter the staffroom!

Continuing support and networking are vital

As with many initiatives that challenge convention, it can be difficult to maintain momentum and resist self-doubt and opposition, both subtle and explicit. Experience suggests that it is valuable to develop networks of schools and staff who are in a position to share practice and provide more general support. This also applies within schools, and so there is value in creating opportunities for practitioners to share practice and experiences regularly in a safe and supportive context, and to be reassured that others share their beliefs about the relevance of Restorative Approaches.

Sustainability needs to be built in

Finally, and it perhaps goes without saying, the development and mainte-nance of Restorative Approaches will not be a smooth curve. Rather, it will enjoy success and meet challenges – some practical, some attitudinal – that will test the resolve and commitment of practitioners. But as Restorative Practice develops, so schools change, and the model adopted needs to be dynamic enough to change also – meeting the needs of the school as a learn-ing and growing organization while staying true to the basic principles of a restorative value base. There is now growing and compelling evidence (see Chapter 2) that this is both achievable and effective.

We will leave the last words in this chapter to a headteacher who has experi-ence of managing Restorative Practice development in her school since 2005:

What have been the biggest challenges in implementing Restorative Approaches?
  'Initially, a feeling of children "getting away" with inappropriate behav-iour and a [perceived] need for "punishment" were the main barriers to the process being seen as acceptable. Staff were uncomfortable with the notion that children could resolve the conflict and agree on what needed to happen to repair the harm as they [staff] had long-established experience of being the people responsible for deciding how any matter should be resolved.'

What have been the most positive outcomes of implementation?
  'Children were very quick to embrace the new way of working as they felt comfortable with the fact that they knew this process meant everyone got to tell their story. When aggressive incidents took place in school, children calmed down much more readily, knowing that the matter would be resolved restoratively. This meant all parties would be accountable for the incident rather than the aggressor being punished.... The children are more confident in sharing their feelings and in accepting responsibility for their part in any conflict.'

What advice would you give to a senior management team at a school about to embark on implementation of Restorative Approaches?
  'Be brave! If you believe in this process then it will work.... You need to be a model of good practice and operate restoratively in how you manage your school. Invite people to share their experiences with you and your staff. Train everyone and be prepared for the negative responses, but don't waver from your vision.'

Restorative approaches: a self-evaluation toolkit for schools

(Reproduced with the permission of Fife Council Education Service)

Developing Restorative Approaches in schools represents in some ways a significant departure from well-established methods of dealing with indiscipline, misbehaviour and relationship difficulties. Historically, approaches to managing such concerns have developed from a punishment-based model. Although recent years have witnessed a significant shift towards more positive approaches, there is little doubt of the currency of view in secondary schools that the primary response to unacceptable or inappropriate behaviour should be negative.

Restorative Approaches in education have been developing in Scotland over the past three years as the result of a government-funded pilot programme involving Fife, North Lanarkshire and Highland Councils. Although each of the authorities has taken a slightly different approach to development, a clear set of core principles are shared. These derive from the original pioneering application of Restorative Practice within criminal justice settings, and can be summarized as an approach to offending and inappropriate behaviour that puts the repairing of harm done to relationships and people over and above the need for assigning blame and dispensing punishment.

This approach can represent a real challenge to more traditional views, and research clearly indicates that the successful adoption and development of Restorative Practice within an organization are crucially dependent on the prevailing ethos and culture. This research and local experience consistently indicate four key factors that impact directly on an organization's readiness to adopt Restorative Approaches. The purpose of this self-evaluation instrument is to make schools aware of these factors, enable them to relate them to areas of existing effective practice, and identify possible areas for development to ensure the creation of a receptive culture.

Central to the adoption of Restorative Approaches is the principle that all members of the organization or community need to have a sense of involvement, and that there should be some broad commonly held values within the organization that are consistent with a Restorative Approach.

Schools are, of course, complex organizations made up of a range of individuals, and it is unlikely that all staff agree about everything – especially something as potentially controversial and challenging as Restorative Approaches. However, we believe that the process of seeking staff views about the key factors will engage and involve staff in the development, and clearly identify areas where further preparatory work might need to be undertaken.

There are a number of ways in which the self-evaluation instrument can be used, and you will know which one will be best for your school. For example, it can be used as a straightforward questionnaire, with the collated results forming the basis of a feedback and planning activity.

Alternatively, the questions can be used as a basis for discussion, again with action points being noted. This can be done as a whole school or as groups, with feedback being collated and analyzed. For example, the results of the self-evaluation may indicate a particular department or team within the school that shows clear evidence of 'readiness'.

Research has shown that initial development of Restorative Approaches on a small scale within a large organization can be a particularly effective way to implement a change in culture over time, so this team or department may well serve as the starting point from which to develop and embed Restorative Approaches across a secondary school.

In considering the readiness of the school community to adopt Restorative Approaches, it may also be helpful to consider additional evidence that would indicate an openness to cultural and relational change. In all of these activities it can be very helpful to enlist the help of a 'critical friend' who will ask insightful and challenging questions about the views generated.

This self-evaluation model is of course underpinned by the three key questions referred to in *How Good Is Our School?* (HMIE Scotland 2007):

- How are we doing?
- How do we know?
- What are we going to do now?

Whichever method is adopted, the key aim is to arrive at a genuine picture of where the school is in relation to a number of key areas that we know relate to how effectively Restorative Approaches can be developed and sustained across the whole school.

The pages that follow contain the self-evaluation toolkit (Figures 8.2–8.5). It can be used in whatever way you consider best for your own school.

These processes are central to Restorative Approaches, and while schools will be very familiar with all of them there is a need to explore in some detail how staff understand them, and how skilled they feel in their application.

Key questions:

1. Meetings are a valuable opportunity to problem solve.

Agree	Not sure	Disagree

2. Meetings about difficult topics always generate emotions; these should be acknowledged and dealt with in the meeting.

Agree	Not sure	Disagree

3. I possess effective skills in managing, contributing to and supporting others in meetings.

Agree	Not sure	Disagree

4. It's helpful to analyze and reflect on the outcome of meetings, especially difficult ones, afterwards.

Agree	Not sure	Disagree

Areas for development, and proposed action:

Figure 8.2 Self-evaluation toolkit. Factor 1: meetings, communication, agreements

Source: Reproduced with the permission of Fife Council Education Service.

A fundamental principle of Restorative Approaches centres on the benefits of offering genuine, sincere apologies for behaviour, and, where appropriate, undertaking some form of reparation. Additionally, the belief that children and young people can change their behaviour is a cornerstone of the approach.

Key questions:

1. A genuine apology is an opportunity for all involved in an incident or a situation to move on.

Agree	Not sure	Disagree

2. Children can be supported to gain better understanding of their behaviour and its consequences, and what to do to make things better.

Agree	Not sure	Disagree

3. Making reparation is a useful process in resolving difficult incidents or situations.

Agree	Not sure	Disagree

4. Children's behaviour can change.

Agree	Not sure	Disagree

Areas for development, and proposed action:

Figure 8.3 Self-evaluation toolkit. Factor 2: apologies, reparation, behaviour change

Source: Reproduced with the permission of Fife Council Education Service.

Human beings are social animals, and seek relationships and involvement with others. Responses to unacceptable behaviour sometimes involve the social exclusion of those who have misbehaved. A Restorative perspective suggests that this approach rarely brings about effective long-term change in behaviour, and is more likely to be counter-productive.

Key questions:

1. Social inclusion encourages the development of acceptable behaviour and attitudes.

Agree	Not sure	Disagree

2. Membership of social groups is important to children, even when they find this difficult.

Agree	Not sure	Disagree

3. Children who are struggling to participate in social groups can be supported to do this more effectively.

Agree	Not sure	Disagree

4. Punishment, criticism and social exclusion can have negative consequences, and may act against positive long-term change.

Agree	Not sure	Disagree

Areas for development, and proposed action:

Figure 8.4 Self-evaluation toolkit. Factor 3: social integration

Source: Reproduced with the permission of Fife Council Education Service.

Schools are complex organisations in which issues like relationships and behaviour have a widespread impact, both on a day-to-day basis and in terms of the development of ethos or culture. The value of consistency of policy and practice across schools in key areas, such as behaviour management, is now well understood, as is the contribution that everyone has to make in developing these.

Key questions:

1. All staff contribute meaningfully to the development and review of effective policies and practice regarding behaviour and relationships.

Agree	Not sure	Disagree

2. School staff are supported in the development of key skills in managing behaviour and relationships.

Agree	Not sure	Disagree

3. Staff feel valued and supported.

Agree	Not sure	Disagree

4. Staff model positive social relationships and behaviour.

Agree	Not sure	Disagree

Areas for development, and proposed action:

Figure 8.5 Self-evaluation toolkit. Factor 4: whole-school involvement

Source: Reproduced with the permission of Fife Council Education Service.

Author's afterword: the past, consequences and future

The Past

Hi, Richard. Can you tell me what happened?

'When I started out as a science teacher I felt I was quite good at forming positive relationships with most of the children. But I used to get very frustrated at times when people behaved inappropriately because I didn't have many successful ways of supporting them and helping them to change their behaviour. Sometimes I got quite angry, but giving out punishments didn't seem to help, and I was never comfortable with that approach anyway.'

So you felt there was a tension between how you wanted to work with the children and how you were expected to deal with misbehaviour?

'Yes, that's it.'

What happened next?

'After eight years of class teaching I moved into a support for learning role, working with children experiencing social, emotional and behavioural difficulties. Over the next twelve years I learned about a range of Restorative Approaches and gradually introduced these into my practice.'

How did you feel using these approaches?

'I was much happier, for a number of reasons. The approaches sat more comfortably with how I wanted to work with children, seeing them as whole people and not just looking at their behaviours. More importantly, these approaches seemed to give the children a real opportunity to reflect on their behaviour and to change it for the better.'

The consequences

Who was affected by these changes?

'Well, I was, because I felt I had at last found ways of working that could make a difference for all children, including those who faced the greatest difficulties in their lives. My work became much more satisfying and rewarding.'

How were the children affected?

'They seemed to appreciate that their concerns were being taken seriously – that they were being listened to – and this seemed to help them understand their own behaviours better. For some, change was a slow process but for others this was the starting point for dramatic and positive changes in their lives.'

Was anyone else affected?

'I know some staff were. They began to see the possible benefits of Restorative Approaches as well – particularly those who participated in some of the processes with children who had been difficult, or even abusive, with them. At least, they reported that they were satisfied with the outcomes and that relationships could be improved. But I still got frustrated, because I could see the potential *but didn't have an opportunity to see it put into practice across the whole school.*'

The Future

So what needs to happen now for things to be put right?

'I think there are a number of things that could make a difference. I really regret the missed opportunities I had to work more positively with children when I first taught in schools. I knew punishing them wasn't helping but I thought I was doing the best I could with what I had. Knowing what I know now, I wish I could have some of that time back.

'I think all teachers and parents need to hear about Restorative Practice. It's not a panacea for society's ills, nor is it a quick fix for all school problems. But it does, perhaps for the first time in the recent history of schooling, offer a proactive and positive way of working that can help us all, children and adults, to take a bit more responsibility for our actions, to understand better how we affect other people and to work together better.

'I think education services and governmental education departments need to take a serious look at what a really coherent approach to Restorative Practice could achieve – not just for our schools, but for our wider communities as well.'

Specifically, what could you do to try to ensure things get better?

'Well, I've been pondering that question for a number of years now. I've worked with children, school staff and school managers. I've trained children and staff and worked with whole schools to implement Restorative Practice. This has been really rewarding work. What else could I do to widen its scope? Perhaps I could write a book?'

And what else could people be doing in the future that would make a difference?

'Well, I think that's down to you, the reader. If you have yet to embark on the Restorative Practice journey, then I hope this book will have opened the gate that leads to that road. If you are already some way down the road, then I hope this book has given you some useful ideas and opportunities to reflect on your own practice. If I can revisit my driving analogy one last time, we are not born knowing how to drive. But with good tutoring, the right information and a helpful guidebook we can learn to navigate to new lands that offer up exciting possibilities. I wish you well on the journey.'

Resources

General

Just Schools: A Whole School Approach to Restorative Justice (2004) Belinda Hopkins. Jessica Kingsley Publishers, London.

Restorative Practices in Classrooms: Rethinking Behaviour Management (2004) Margaret Thorsborne and David Vinegrad. Incentive Publishing, Milton Keynes.

The Little Book of Restorative Justice (2002) Howard Zehr. Good Books, Intercourse, PA.

Proactive approaches

Being Cool in School and *What's Going On?* Health and Wellbeing (PSHE) curricular programme for ages 4-14. Fife Council Education Service.

Peer support

Peer Support in Action: From Bystanding to Standing By (2000) Helen Cowie and Patti Wallace. Sage Publications, London.

Restorative Interventions

Restorative Practices and Bullying (2008) Margaret Thorsborne and David Vinegrad. Speechmark Publishing, Milton Keynes.

Bullying: A Complete Guide to the Support Group Method (2008) George Robinson and Barbara Maines. Sage Publications, London.

Person-centred theory

Freedom to Learn, 3rd edn (1994) Carl R. Rogers and H. Jerome Freiberg. Merrill/Macmillan, Columbus, OH.

Internet resources

Note: an asterisk indicates that the organization is a commercial one.

Sacro (Safeguarding Communities and Reducing Conflict):
www.sacro.org.uk

Scottish Mediation Network: www.scottishmediation.org.uk

Peer Mediation Network: www.peermediationnetwork.org.uk

Leap Confronting Conflict: www.leaplinx.com

*Margaret Thorsborne and Associates: www.thorsborne.com.au

*Transforming Conflict (National Centre for Restorative Justice in
   Education): www.transformingconflict.org

*International Institute for Restorative Practices:
   www.safersanerschools.org

*Quality Circle Time: www.circle-time.co.uk

References

Bitel, M. (2005) *National Evaluation of the Restorative Justice In Schools Programme*, Youth Justice Board for England and Wales, London.

Blood, P. and Thorsborne, M. (2005) 'The challenge of culture change', Paper presented to the Sixth International Conference on Conferencing, Circles and Other Restorative Practices, Sydney, Australia, March 3–5, 2005.

Braithwaite, J. (1989) *Crime, Shame and Reintegration*, Cambridge University Press.

Brookes, D. (2005) 'Restorative Practices for Schools: Manual for Facilitators' (unpublished), Scottish Restorative Justice Consultancy and Training Service/Sacro.

Cameron, L. and Thorsborne, M. (1999) 'Restorative justice and school discipline: mutually exclusive?' In H. Strang and J. Braithwaite (eds) *Restorative Justice and Civil Society*, Cambridge University Press, Cambridge.

Cameron, L. and Thosborne, M. (2001) 'Restorative justice and school discipline: mutually exclusive?' In H. Strang and J. Braithwaite (Eds) *Restorative Justice and Civil Society*, Cambridge University Press, Cambridge.

Clutterbuck, D. (2008) www.scottishmentoringnetwork.co.uk/defaultpage121c0.aspx?pageID=16. Accessed 20th September 2008.

Douglas, T. (2000) *Basic Groupwork* 2nd edn, Routledge, London.

Drewery, W. (2004) *Restorative Practices in Schools*, University of Wakaito, Hamilton, New Zealand.

Durlak, J.A., Weissberg, R.P., Dymnicki, A.B., Taylor, R.D. and Schellinger, K. (2008) *The Effects of Social and Emotional Learning on the Behavior and Academic Performance of School Children*, CASEL, University of Illinois at Chicago. Available at www.casel.org/downloads/ASP-Full.pdf (accessed 03 June 2008).

Dwivedi, K. (1993) *Group Work with Children and Adolescents: A Handbook*, Jessica Kingsley, London.

Glasser, W. (1969) *Schools without Failure*, Harper & Row, New York.

HMIE Scotland (2007) *How Good Is Our School? The Journey to Excellence*, Her Majesty's Inspectorate of Education, Livingston.

Hoyle, C., Young, R. and Hill, R. (2002) *Proceed with Caution: An Evaluation of the Thames Valley Police Initiative in Restorative Cautioning*, Joseph Rowntree Foundation, York.

Kane, J., Lloyd, G., McCluskey, G., Riddell, S., Stead, J. and Weedon, E. (2007) *An Evaluation of 'Restorative Practices in Three Scottish Councils'*, Scottish Executive Education Department, Edinburgh.

Kelly, P. and Colquhoun, D. (2005) 'The professionalisation of stress management: health and wellbeing as a professional duty of care?', *Critical Public Health* 15(2), 135–145.

Marsh, P. and Crowe, G. (1998) *Family Group Conferences in Child Welfare*, Blackwell, Oxford.

Marshall, T. (1998) *Standards for Restorative Justice*, Restorative Justice Consortium, London.

Marshall, T. (1999) *Restorative Justice: An Overview*, Home Office Occasional Paper, Home Office, London.

McCold, P. (1996) Restorative Justice and the role of the community, in Galaway, B. and Hudson, J. (eds) *Restorative Justice: International Perspectives*, Criminal Justice Press, New York.

McCold, P. and Wachtel, T. (2003) *In Pursuit of Paradigm: A Theory of Restorative Justice*, www.restorativepractices.org/library/paradigm.html (accessed 2 May 2008)

McGillis, D. (1997) *Community Mediation Programs: Developments and Challenges, Issues and Practices*, US Department of Justice, Washington, DC.

McGrath, J. (2004) *Restorative Practices in Education: Managing Challenging Behaviour*, Evaluation Report for Southend-on-Sea, Netcare Consultancy, Newry.

Moore, D.B. and O'Connell, T. (1994) 'Family conferencing in Wagga Wagga: a communitarian model of justice'. In C. Alder and J. Wundersitz (eds) *Family Conferencing and Juvenile Justice: The Way Forward or Misplaced Optimism?*, Australian Institute of Criminology, Canberra.

Morrison, B. (2002) 'Bullying and victimisation in schools: a restorative justice approach', *Trends and Issues in Crime and Criminal Justice*, no. 219, Australian Institute of Criminology, February.

Morrison, B. (2007) *Restoring Safe School Communities*, Willan, Cullompton.

Moseley, J. (2003) *Turn Your School Around*, Learning Development Aids, Wisbech.

Munn, P., Lloyd, G. and Cullen, M.A. (2000) *Alternatives to Exclusion from School*, Paul Chapman, London.

Munn, P., Sharpe, S. and Johnstone, M. (2004) *Discipline in Scottish Schools*, Scottish Executive Education Department, Edinburgh.

Nathanson, D.L. (1992) *Shame and Pride*, W.W. Norton, New York.

Parsons, C. (2005) 'School exclusion: the will to punish', *British Journal of Educational Studies* 53(2), 187–211.

Porter, A. (2005) *Restorative Practices at Queanbeyan South, an Australian Primary School*, available at www.restorativejustice.org/articlesdb/articles/5877 (accessed 2 May 2008).

Preston, N. (2002) *Restorative Justice: A New School of Thought*, Thames Valley Partnership, London.

Sherman, L. and Strang, H. (1997) *Restorative Justice and Deterring Crime*, RISE Working Papers, Australian National University.

Smith, L. and Hennessy, J. (1999) *Making a Difference: Essex Family Group Conference Project, Research Findings and Practice Issues*, Essex County Council, Chelmsford.

Van Ness, D. and Strong, K. (2002) *Restoring Justice*, 2nd edn, Anderson Publishing, Cincinnati, OH.

Wachtel, T. (2004) *Restorative Practices Build Community, Responsibility*, www.educationworld.com/a_issues/chat/chat093.html (accessed 2 May 2008).

Wachtel, T. (2005) *'Creating safer saner schools through Restorative Practices'*, Paper presented to the to XIV World Congress of Criminology, Philadelphia, PA.

Walgrave, L. (ed.) (2003) *Repositioning Restorative Justice*, Willan, Cullompton.

Ylvislaker, M. and Feeney, T.J. (1998) *Collaborative Brain Injury Intervention*, Singular Publishing Group, London.

Zehr, H. (1985) 'Retributive justice, restorative justice', *New Perspectives on Crime and Justice*, issue 4, Mennonite Central Committee Office of Criminal Justice, Akron, PA.

Zehr, H. (1990) *Changing Lenses: A New Focus for Crime and Justice*, Herald Press, Scottsdale, PA.

Zehr, H. (2002) *The Little Book of Restorative Justice*, Good Books, Intercourse, PA.

Index